# Offerings

# Offerings

*Thoughts on What Matters Most*

## BYRON PAUL BROUGHT

Copyright © 2014 Byron Paul Brought.

All rights reserved. No part of this book may be used or reproduced by any means, graphic, electronic, or mechanical, including photocopying, recording, taping or by any information storage retrieval system without the written permission of the publisher except in the case of brief quotations embodied in critical articles and reviews.

WestBow Press books may be ordered through booksellers or by contacting:

WestBow Press
A Division of Thomas Nelson & Zondervan
1663 Liberty Drive
Bloomington, IN 47403
www.westbowpress.com
1 (866) 928-1240

Because of the dynamic nature of the Internet, any web addresses or links contained in this book may have changed since publication and may no longer be valid. The views expressed in this work are solely those of the author and do not necessarily reflect the views of the publisher, and the publisher hereby disclaims any responsibility for them.

Certain stock imagery © Thinkstock.
Any people depicted in stock imagery provided by Thinkstock are models, and such images are being used for illustrative purposes only.

New Revised Standard Version Bible, copyright © 1989, Division of Christian Education of the National Council of the Churches of Christ in the United States of America. Used by permission. All rights reserved.

ISBN: 978-1-4908-3743-7 (e)
ISBN: 978-1-4908-3742-0 (sc)
ISBN: 978-1-4908-3741-3 (hc)

Library of Congress Control Number: 2014908804

Printed in the United States of America.

WestBow Press rev. date: 5/20/2014

To
the memory of
Jane Raffensperger Brought and Byron Vance Brought Jr.,
and with gratitude to
Mary Kay Cammack Brought,
who in their lives have demonstrated
unconditional love

# ✻ Order of Offerings

Prologue ........................................................................................ xi

Prayer ............................................................................................. 1
The Refrigerator ............................................................................ 1
Geese .............................................................................................. 2
Don't Wait ..................................................................................... 3
Grand ............................................................................................. 4
Tourists .......................................................................................... 5
Voices ............................................................................................. 8
Let Go .......................................................................................... 10
No and Yes ................................................................................... 11
The Warning ............................................................................... 12
Consequences .............................................................................. 15
Why the Seventh? ....................................................................... 17
The Option .................................................................................. 19
It Is Good .................................................................................... 21
Words ........................................................................................... 22
The Cantaloupe ........................................................................... 24
The Eagle ..................................................................................... 25
Roots ............................................................................................ 27
Patrick .......................................................................................... 29
The Garden ................................................................................. 31
The River ..................................................................................... 32
First Diversion ............................................................................. 34
A Projection? ............................................................................... 38
The Fool ....................................................................................... 40
Just Take No for an Answer ....................................................... 42
Choose ......................................................................................... 44
How Sad ...................................................................................... 45
The Question .............................................................................. 46
An Open Letter to People of Faith ............................................ 47

| | |
|---|---|
| An Open Letter to All Who Do Not Believe in God | 49 |
| Where Was God? | 51 |
| Power | 54 |
| Plaster | 55 |
| The Moron | 57 |
| Time | 58 |
| The Leaf | 60 |
| Take a Walk | 61 |
| Remember | 62 |
| Be Strong | 64 |
| The Apple Tree | 66 |
| Women | 67 |
| The Bird Feeder | 68 |
| Holy War | 69 |
| The Work of Religion | 70 |
| Risky Giving | 72 |
| Treasures in Unexpected Places | 75 |
| Second Diversion | 77 |
| Christmas | 83 |
| The Stable | 85 |
| Pleasure and Joy | 85 |
| Seeing God | 87 |
| The Spring | 89 |
| Ethics from the Future | 90 |
| Out of Order | 91 |
| No More! | 92 |
| Open Hands, Softened Hearts | 94 |
| Only Two | 96 |
| The Test | 98 |
| The Mirror | 99 |
| The Changed Sentence | 101 |
| All by Grace | 102 |
| Forgetful | 104 |
| Religious? | 105 |

| | |
|---|---|
| Ugly | 107 |
| Angry | 108 |
| Remember This Night | 110 |
| Too Short | 112 |
| Third Diversion | 113 |
| The Lie | 122 |
| The Hard One | 123 |
| The Fire Alarm | 124 |
| The Proposal | 126 |
| Free to Go | 127 |
| The Well | 129 |
| The Four-Letter Word | 130 |
| Controlled | 130 |
| Unwilling Servants | 132 |
| The Table | 134 |
| Holy Communion | 135 |
| The Stained-Glass Window | 136 |
| The Diamond | 137 |
| Expectations | 138 |
| Two Churches or One? | 139 |
| God in Three Persons | 142 |
| Fourth Diversion | 145 |
| Generous to All | 148 |
| Where is Spain? | 150 |
| Confidence | 152 |
| I Want You to Know | 153 |
| Out of a Tomb | 154 |
| Becoming | 157 |
| The Invitation | 159 |
| From Above | 160 |
| A Day in Early March | 162 |
| Like Christ | 164 |
| Keep the Faith | 165 |
| Daffodils | 166 |

# ✦ Prologue

Some offerings are influential and magnanimous, conveying a power that results in notable and lasting accomplishments. The creation of a scholarship will advance the lives of countless students through its annual distributions and leave a lasting legacy. The philanthropic gift that builds a hospital will create a place where the sick are healed and the broken made whole, in the present and in the future.

Other offerings are paltry and small, barely measurable by any normal standards. The writings that follow most assuredly fall into this latter category. I would have preferred to call them *Confessions,* for they represent the accumulated beliefs and experiences of one who has now entered an eighth decade of earthly life. But *Confessions* might falsely imply that these meager offerings might remotely resemble the genius of Augustine or the far-reaching significance of Patrick. Likewise, **Thoughts** might have been a good title, for that is what they are: scattered thoughts and observations, what an old Irishman might call "wee danders through the burrens of life." But in no way can these reflections be compared with the profound insights of Pascal.

Thus, *Offerings*—no more, no less. Offered for perhaps no other reason than that I need to give them. And so I begin, with the uncertain hope that someone, somewhere, will benefit from the reading. Perhaps, like the two small coins a widow once gave at the temple gates, they will bring a warm and accepting smile to the face of the Savior (Luke 21:1–4).

## ✻ Prayer

It is wise to begin any human endeavor with prayer. As Homer began *The Iliad* by invoking the goddess, and as Milton invoked the heavenly muse at the beginning of *Paradise Lost*, so I humbly invoke the Spirit of the living God. If, in God's good time and in God's good way, the answer is in the positive, I would be grateful. But if the answer is no, I shall be content, in the full confidence that God's will ultimately and inevitably will be done.

Lord God, when the world was without form and void, and darkness was upon the face of the deep, your Spirit was moving. You spoke and there was light (Genesis 1:1–3). Move anew, oh God, so that even from the dark and chaotic nothingness of these writings, your light may shine.

## ✻ The Refrigerator

American homes are enhanced with luxuries and conveniences that were unknown to previous generations and even now are unavailable to many in the Third World. Perhaps the most significant of these blessings is an appliance that serves two vitally important functions. The refrigerator not only keeps foods cold, fresh, and free from the rapid growth of harmful bacteria, but it also is the depository of extremely precious treasures and valuables. When I visit in the home of a friend or neighbor, I love to examine their refrigerators, these priceless collections of art and history, attached with simple magnets to the refrigerator door.

There are usually photos there: a daughter, with beautifully coiffed hair and dressed in a stunning gown on the night of her high school prom; a son, handsomely attired on the day he proudly became a United States Marine; a grandchild, wearing the bright blue jersey of a traveling soccer team. Frequently, those photos include a family gathering at a summer vacation beach or on the porch of a mountain cabin. Often, there is artwork on display, as prominent as if it were hung in the Metropolitan: a finger-painted sun shining down on a gray and yellow cow (or is it a dog?), or a colored-pencil drawing of a flower looming in green and red from the dark brown earth. And like the Metropolitan collection, these are pieces of priceless value. Sometimes there is church bulletin or a school newsletter announcing a pancake supper, a choral festival, or a holiday service or concert.

In all the homes I have ever been in and on the doors of all the refrigerators I have ever seen, I have never once seen a bill of currency under a magnet, the picture of a stock certificate, the photo of a gold or silver ingot, the drawing of a costly diamond brooch, or indeed the representation of anything that can be identified with what the Scriptures call "mammon," material wealth and possessions.

What is really important in life? What is it that matters most?

The answer will not be found in the monthly statement from the bank or a brokerage firm.

It will be revealed under a simple magnet on the refrigerator door.

# Geese

There is a time in the shortening days at the end of summer when a vague uneasiness sweeps over the great flocks of Canada geese. Too long they have lived in Canada. The air grows cool about them, the sun goes down a little earlier, and a light frost glistens on the morning grass. Suddenly, with the first dawning of a new day's light, the mighty wings rush downward, and the geese are thrust aloft into the chill September air. High above the ground, they move in a pencil-thin V-formation, their deep-throated *ka-ronk* heralding their arrival before they can be seen.

The geese must live in two different worlds. Their native home is Canada, where they live and breed from the St. Lawrence to the Arctic Circle. They are ideally suited for the crisp, chill days of a Canadian summer, thriving in the cold, clear waters of Ontario and Quebec. But each fall, the geese must journey southward to Maryland and Virginia, wintering along the swampy wetlands of the Chesapeake Bay. The northern winters are too harsh, the food supply too limited, for them to survive. They migrate to warmer shores.

The geese must live in two worlds. If they tried to live in only one, they would perish.

The biblical view of humankind is that we, too, must live in two worlds.

We live, of course, on planet earth, creatures among other creatures, animals in many ways, mammals slightly higher up an evolutionary ladder than apes and monkeys, porpoises and whales. Like all earthly creatures, we must eat, drink water, breathe oxygen, protect ourselves against aggressors, and shelter ourselves from the fury of the elements. That is the world that is so familiar to us, the world where we grow up and go to school, where we get a job and raise a family, where we find happiness and self-fulfillment, and where we know sickness, encounter difficulties, grow old, and die. We live in that world and participate in it.

But we must all live and function in another world: the world of the soul, the world of the Spirit, the world of God. The things of that world are unseen and untouched, but they are real and true—realities like love and righteousness, faith and hope, prayer and worship.

The human race dare not live in only one climate.

Like the great flights of the migratory geese, we must make frequent and periodic journeys to another homeland.

# Don't Wait

There are times when my grandchildren are running through the house and jumping on the sofa that I wish for some peace and quiet. But then I realize that all too soon they will be grown up, too mature to run and jump, and I give thanks for all the noise.

There are times when the sweat is dripping down my face as I mow the lawn that I wish the heat and humidity of summer would be over.

But then I realize that all too soon, another summer will have ended, and I give thanks that I am hot.

How naively we assume that life will go on forever and that things will always be the way they are now. The psalmist brings us back to reality. We are like a dream, like grass that is renewed in the morning, but in the evening it fades and withers (Psalm 90:5–6). Teach us to count our days, the psalmist prays, so that we may gain a wise heart (Psalm 90:12).

To number our days is not to sit around in a morbid depression. It is to gain wisdom. It is to learn a vitally important lesson in life: don't wait.

Don't wait to end an argument. End it before the sun goes down. Tomorrow may be too late.

Don't wait to help someone in need. Help when it is needed, not at your convenience.

Don't wait to hug your children. Hug them today, before they grow up and move away.

Don't wait to love your parents. Tomorrow your parents may be beyond your touch. Show them love today.

Don't wait to turn to God. Don't wait to place your trust in God, to serve God, to dedicate your life to God. Don't wait to seek forgiveness. Don't wait to receive a grace that is freely given. Don't wait to sing a hymn, lift a prayer, or simply look to the heavens and say, "Thank you."

Don't wait.

The time is now.

# Grand

In the predawn twilight they gather, filled with an eager expectation. Some bring lawn chairs as they wait, their anticipation growing as the darkness disappears. You would think a great spectacle is about to take place. And it is. It is sunrise at the Grand Canyon.

The canyon is well named. Eight to ten miles wide, 277 miles long, and one mile deep, it truly is a grand canyon. Standing on its rim is not so much a vacation as it is a spiritual experience. The immensity, the grandeur, the beauty, and the sheer awesome majesty are beyond description.

The sun rises, and light begins to creep down the canyon walls. From dark red and ocher to deep purple hues, the age-old rocks, crevasses, and mesas are bathed in light. The patterns of sunlight change moment by moment until the entire height of the canyon walls is directly illuminated. Each moment reveals new glories, never before seen and never again to be repeated in exactly the same way.

Again at sunset, the crowds will gather to watch, as the shadows lengthen and the sun's rays inch upward on their relentless climb, until darkness descends on the highest ridge and only the moonlight casts a silver glow on the canyon walls. These moments are not to be missed. Sunrise and sunset are sacred moments.

How many sunrises have I slept through? How many sunsets have I been too busy to observe, too distracted by my little agenda to stand in awe? Does not all of creation bear witness to the glory of God? Is not the Creator's grandeur seen in every canyon, on every hilltop, in every valley and every mountain, in every pine forest and every coastline, in every cascade of waterfall, and in every fragile petal of crocus and bluebell?

And in the grandness of every sunrise and sunset?

## Tourists

Many people come each year to visit a place that is unique among the treasures of this world, a place with more photo opportunities than the mind can imagine. It is a place of beauty and majesty, of animals and natural features, of brilliant sunshine and sudden summer snowstorms. It is a place named for the color of the age-old rock formations that border a plunging canyon. It is a place called Yellowstone.

Some visitors arrive from the south, passing the breathtaking magnificence of the Grand Tetons, journeying along the Snake River, and passing waterfalls, lakes, and mountains to a large geyser basin steaming with vapor, including one that faithfully rewards onlookers with what is nearly an hourly eruption.

Some visitors come from the west, departing from a seasonally crowded tourist town to a river warmed year-round by geothermal activity, appropriately named the Firehole. Heading north, they soon pass Gibbon Falls and even more geyser basins at Norris.

Some tourists come from the north, the one entrance open year-round, to hot springs that can only be described by what they are, Mammoth, and southward to massive cliffs of obsidian.

Yet others arrive from the northeast, passing through a Montana town where once Native Americans constructed a red lodge, and then, passing by Hell Roaring Creek, climb steeply skyward through a series of switchbacks to a land where the snow never melts, where one of the jagged peaks resembles a bear's tooth, and where small towns once claimed miners who dreamed of riches from silver and gold.

One such pair of visitors came from the East Entrance on a bus filled with eager tourists, each armed with the wide range of necessary accessories: cameras and iPhones, field glasses and water bottles, and suitcases so stuffed they would cause a pioneer family, riding on a Conestoga wagon, to marvel with envy. As the bus climbed into the park, they drove through Sylvan Pass, surrounded by peaks with the fearful names "Avalanche" and "Grizzly" on either side of the road. Some on the bus were disappointed. From videos they had seen, they had expected to see huge herds of buffalo, packs of roaming wolves, and wandering bears at every bend of the path. But they noticed only a mule deer peacefully grazing in a meadow. Had they stopped at Pelican Creek, they would have seen moose foraging water reeds in the wetlands, but the bus driver hurried on his scheduled way. They crossed over the Fishing Bridge, where the Yellowstone River emerges from Yellowstone Lake, with waters that will mingle with the Missouri, the Mississippi, and the Gulf of Mexico.

The first stop gave the passengers the chance to stretch their legs and experience the sulfur cauldron, where the Mud Volcano cooks and bubbles like a giant pot of oatmeal boiling over on the stove, where dead trees stand limbless in a lake called "Sour," and where the odor of hydrogen sulfide hangs heavily in the air. Our two tourists were struck by the unearthly landscape but quickly returned to the comfort of the bus, where one of them sent a hasty text: "OMG, the stench is dreadful."

Heading northward, the bus now passed through Hayden Valley, where passengers did see bison, much to their delight. Had they lingered longer and observed more closely, they would have seen pelicans floating on the river and swallows darting over the water. They came to a popular tourist stop, Grand Canyon of the Yellowstone. Standing on the canyon's rim, travelers share an awesome moment: seeing the sunlight play on yellow, amber, and orange canyon walls and hearing the subdued roar of the surging water far below, as it drops 308 feet over the Lower Falls. Our couple emerged from the bus and took numerous photos. But they especially enjoyed the gift shop, where one can purchase small bears stuffed by Chinese workers, and sweatshirts of every size and color stamped "Yellowstone."

When the tour ended, and the couple returned home, they were frequently asked, "How was your vacation?" "It was a wonderful trip," they answered, "but wasn't it a shame that the cabins had no television?"

Years earlier, another tourist had come to Yellowstone. A young man of twenty years, he came "to see the West" and to earn some college money by working in a service station. In those bygone years, attendants pumped your gas, washed your windshield, and checked your oil. This tourist traversed much of same area that our previously mentioned couple had visited, although he did not go by bus. Over the span of that summer, now so long ago, he hiked along the river, climbed the peak called Avalanche, watched the moose graze among the water plants, stood quietly among the towering trunks of lodge pole pine, sat amid a meadow of lupine and paintbrush, and spent long hours by the lakeside, where the only sound is the gentle ripple of wavelets on the shore. Away from the tourists and the traffic and the commercial transactions of the gift shop and the service station, he spent much time alone—completely and utterly alone.

But he was not alone, not at any moment alone. For there, in the silence, in the beauty, in the awe-full magnificence, there was a Presence. No burning bush, no commanding voice, no apparition of a form, but a

Presence deeply felt. If you had asked him to describe this Presence, he could not have done so, for words would have failed him. But he felt an awareness of the transcendent, the beyond, the infinite conveyed in the wisp of spruce and fir, in the fragile complexity of the wild iris and the larkspur, in the granites weathered by the frosts and rains of eons, in the stillness of the forest, and in the snow-capped mountains rising across the lake. Eternal grace can be conveyed in bread and wine, and for this young man, it was imparted through one of the Creator's greatest masterpieces: Yellowstone. It was no longer a park, recreational as it might be, but a sacred place, as sacred as the greatest cathedrals of Europe, as holy as the most venerated of ancient scrolls. And all around him, there was nothing made by man. All that he could say in those sacred moments was a simple gasp—not the casually bandied abbreviation of a text message but a response from deep within a creature's heart—"Oh, my God!"

There are many who come to the park. All will come as tourists; some will leave as pilgrims. All will experience great pleasure; some will experience the divine.

Is this not true of life, of all us passing tourists in this earthly park we call our home?

## ❀ Voices

Many, many voices surround us every day. Some voices are from the outside world: radio, television, telephone, the workplace, the street corners, and the classroom; voices from neighbors, friends, and family. Some of these outside voices share information, some ask, some demand, and some just jabber away. But all of them seek our attention.

Other voices come from within, the voices we speak to ourselves. *I'm running late. I wonder what he/she will think of me? Now where did I put my car keys? Lord, help me through this day (this test, this traffic light, this whatever).* Some of these internal voices are detrimental and unhealthy. *I can't do it. I am too old. I'm not strong enough, or rich enough, or well enough. I'm tired. I'm overwhelmed.* In extreme cases, these internal voices can be destructive or suicidal. When you talk to yourself, you need to be careful about what you say. You may become what you say you are.

In the midst of all these voices that we hear each day—all the outside voices and all the voices that we say to ourselves—there is yet another kind of voice. This voice is often drowned out by all the distracting voices that cry out so loudly. It is "a sound of sheer silence," to use the language of Scripture (1 Kings 19:12), a still small voice, a voice of gentle stillness, the voice of a quiet whisper. It is a voice speaking to us that says something like this: "I love you. I care about you. I created you. I made you in my image. I took you from the dust of the earth and breathed into you the breath of life (Genesis 2:7). I have a purpose for your life. I ask that you love me with all your heart and soul and mind, and that you love your neighbor as yourself (Matthew 22:37–39). I require that you do justice, love kindness, and walk humbly before me (Micah 6:8). I will be your God and you shall be my son, my daughter (Jeremiah 31:33b). In my presence there is fullness of joy, and at my right hand are pleasures forevermore (Psalm 16:17).

"Oh, and one more thing: you are never along, for I am with you always, even to the end of the age (Matthew 28:20b). Nothing, not even death, can separate you from my love (Romans 8:38–39); nothing can take away or destroy my ultimate purpose for your life."

When I am feeling sorry for myself and having my own private pity party, I need to hear that voice calling me to calm down, assuring me that everything will be okay. When I am bitter and full of resentment, I need to hear that voice, summoning me to release my anger and to be at peace. When I am following the wrong desire, I need to hear that voice urging me to turn around and take the higher road. And when I am lost in shame and guilt, I need to hear that voice of mercy, accept the grace that can be found in every moment, and be able to forgive myself.

A voice of sheer silence is speaking to us. It is the voice of God.

Can you hear it?

Are you even listening?

# Let Go

Let go. More than good advice, it is a command of the living God. And God is not kidding. Let go.

Let go of the hurt, the anger, the bitterness, the desire for revenge. Let it go. Get rid of it. Give it forth. That is the literal meaning of forgive, to give forth. To forgive is to give forth any and all of the resentment that may be residing deep down inside. That is true in German as well. *Vergeben* (*geben*, give; plus *ver*, forth) means to give it up, to let it go, to get it out of your life.

Resentment is like a poison, a toxin that eats away within us. The word resent comes from the Latin *sentire*, which means to feel. Our English words sentiment and sensuous are derived from it. To resent is to feel again, to feel the hurt and pain all over again. It is to continue to be victimized by whatever wrong or evil was done against you. It is to feel the blood pressure rise, the stomach acid churn, the headache begin. Stop playing the victim. You may have been a victim once, but you do not need to be a victim forever. Release it. Do yourself a favor, and let the poison go.

To forgive does not mean that we camouflage a wrong or somehow pretend that the wrong did not happen. It is not putting a false label on an evil deed or redefining a hurtful word. No, an evil act is still an evil act; a hurtful word is still a hurtful word; and the pain that you felt (and still feel) was really painful. Forgiveness means you do not let a wrong destroy the possibility of a restored and healthy relationship. You do not permit the past to determine the future.

You may not be able to bring about reconciliation, for it takes two to reconcile. The other party must work at it also. But it only takes one to forgive. While you may not be able to change the attitude of another person, you can change your own attitude and make sure that your own heart is in the right place. "If it is possible, so far as it depends on you, live peaceably with all" (Romans 12:18).

"Do not let the sun go down on your anger" (Ephesians 4:26). Do not let a day end with anger and bitterness in your heart.

Let go. And do it before the sun goes down.

# No and Yes

Holy? Yes, holy. That is precisely the description, both of the people of Israel (Exodus 19:6) and of the Christian Church (1 Peter 2:9).

I don't want to be holy. Holy is not my thing. I rebel against the sanctimonious smugness of narrow-minded religion. I certainly do not want to be like the Sunni imam who incites his congregation to violence, or the fundamentalist American preacher who leads his church to picket the funeral of a man who died of AIDS, or the Northern Ireland fanatic who proclaims the evils of popery. A rigid and pious self-righteousness in a religion devoid of love is, for me and for many, a total turnoff. Holy? Forget about it.

But to be holy means none of the above generalizations. They are perversions of the holy, not manifestations of it. To be holy is to set apart for God and to be consecrated to God and God's purposes. A sanctuary is "holy." It is not used as a playground, or a casino, or a marketplace, or an ice-skating rink, or any other secular purpose. It is set apart for God. A communion chalice is "holy." It is not used to serve a cola drink, or a lemonade, or a sweet tea. It is used to share the wine that signifies the blood of Christ.

To be holy is to belong to God. We go through our lives, assuming that we do not belong to anyone or perhaps that we belong only to ourselves. But ultimately, we belong to God; we are his. To be holy is to understand that and to act upon it. To be holy is to realize that without God, we are separated from that to which we really belong. Apart from God, we lack the primary purpose for our existence and are empty and hollow, like a straw-filled scarecrow, standing alone in a vast field.

Anyone can be holy when consecrated for God. The farmer digging in the dirt can be holy. The steelworker sweating over a blast furnace can be holy. The taxi driver stuck in a traffic jam can be holy. The office worker straining in front of a computer screen can be holy. The restaurant worker scrubbing the kitchen floor can be holy. To truly understand that we belong to God and that we are created by God and for God's purpose is to accept a new identity. It is to be holy.

It is not a matter of believing that God exists, in the sense of accepting that somehow, somewhere, there is a supreme reality. It means nothing to say "I believe in God" and to do nothing about it. A God who exists and who does not matter is no better that a God who does not exist at all. If God exists, God must make a difference. If God is real, we had better do something about it. The question is not, "What must I do to be holy?"; it is, "Since I am holy, what must I do?"

To be holy is to say no to certain behaviors and activities. As people who belong to God, there are times when we must say no. We must say no to dishonesty and all words and acts of deception. We must say no to all forms of exploitation and oppression. We must say no to racism and sexism, to prejudice and hatred. We must say no to politicians who look after their own interests while the needs of the poor go unfulfilled. We must say no to some things we have grown accustomed to, such as aimlessly watching trash on television when we could be putting our minds to better use; casually accepting unacceptably low wages for jobs that, while menial, serve a helpful purpose; or ignoring the hungry and homeless in our midst.

And we must say yes. We must say yes to truth and integrity; yes to mercy and justice; yes to persons and institutions that are improving the environment; yes to a spirit of love, peace, and reconciliation in a vengeance-filled world; yes to God, who makes all things new and for whom nothing in impossible; yes to love; yes to life; yes to a new creation. And yes to being holy.

# ✣ The Warning

Warnings are given for a reason. Warnings reveal a danger that any intelligent person will take seriously. Failure to heed a warning may result in personal injury or perhaps even the loss of life.

Look both ways before you cross the street. Don't touch the stove; it is very hot. School Crossing—Speed Limit 30. The Surgeon General has determined that cigarette smoking is dangerous to your health.

To ignore any of these warnings is to take an unnecessary risk, a risk that may well lead to a tragic outcome.

Yet warnings are frequently ignored. Smokers continue to smoke. Children do run into the street. Drivers often exceed the posted speed limit. How strange that folks who otherwise would act in a reasonable and rational way seem oblivious to dangerous conditions.

Whole societies ignore warnings. Scientists clearly and consistently predict that the unrestrained use of fossil fuels will result both in severe weather and rising ocean levels. The warning is virtually ignored, even though climate change threatens the well-being of millions. Concerned parents and school officials call for legislation that sensibly requires a background check before a criminal or a mentally disturbed individual may purchase a gun. The warning is not only ignored, but it is ridiculed.

Why are warnings ignored? Perhaps it is ignorance. Perhaps it is rebellion. Perhaps it is resistance to change. Perhaps it stems from the naïve assumption, "It will not happen to me." Whatever the cause, it is a proud and arrogant people who frivolously or willfully disregard the very warnings that are designed to protect health, happiness, and the common good.

So it is with a stern and solemn warning that has been handed down for thousands of years:

> Take care that you do not forget the LORD your God, by failing to keep his commandments, his ordinances, and his statutes, which I am commanding you today. When you have eaten your fill and have built fine houses and live in them, and when your herds and flocks have multiplied, and your silver and gold is multiplied, and all that you have is multiplied, that you do not exalt yourself, forgetting the LORD your God, who brought you out of the land of Egypt, out of the house of slavery ... Do not say to yourself, "My power and the might of my own hand have gotten me this wealth" (Deuteronomy 8:11–14, 17).

While written as a warning to the people of Israel, surely these words are directed to our own time and our own nations. We have eaten and are full. We have built nice homes and live in them, complete with luxuries that people of previous generations could scarcely imagine and that poverty stricken communities can barely comprehend. Our herds and our flocks have multiplied. Our silver and gold has multiplied. Indeed, all that we have has multiplied. It is true. It is all true. And is it not true that we have forgotten the source of our blessings, that we have proudly assumed that our wealth is the result of our cunning and our labors? Is it not true that, like a patient suffering from dementia who can remember not who he is or where he has come from, we have forgotten the One from whom all blessings flow and to whom we ultimately belong?

It is true. It is all true. Can any other conclusion be made when a people, so intent on getting more and more, devote even a day of national thanksgiving as a jump-start on Black Friday, rushing headlong to the mall and standing for hours in the early morning darkness? Or, like a swarm of lemmings scurrying to the cliffs, push and fight their way to be the first to stampede through the opening doors of whatever establishment has the latest mobile phone at a discount?

For Deuteronomy, the warning is not to be taken lightly; it is a matter of life or death:

"If you forget the LORD your God and follow other gods to serve and worship them, I solemnly warn you today that you shall surely perish" (Deuteronomy 8:19).

When a people forget God, they automatically turn to the pursuit of the lesser gods. Lesser deities receive the devotion and homage. Lesser values become the goal and purpose of existence. And when that happens, the people perish. They are like a mountain climber, climbing up a slippery slope. The climber may be making good time, may think the footing is sure, and may be rejoicing in the ascent. But suddenly, the foot may slip on the icy slope, the climber may crash downward to certain destruction, and the old words of the palmist may come to fulfillment:

"Truly you set them in slippery places; you make them fall to ruin. How they are destroyed in a moment, swept away utterly by terrors!" (Psalm 73:18–19).

A good parent must discipline an unruly child—yes, even a child who, though surrounded by toys, remains ungrateful, wretched, feisty, and self-centered. A good parent must discipline. But before the discipline, a good parent will issue a warning. And if the child has any sense at all, he or she will heed it.

Take care that you do not forget the Lord your God.

Do not say to yourself, "My power and the might of my own hand have gotten me this wealth."

If you forget the Lord your God, you shall surely perish.

The warning has been given.

## Consequences

Relativism speaks with a loud voice in the postmodern world. Truth is relative. Morality is relative. There is no universal goodness, and there is no universal value. What I consider to be right is what I have defined as being right. It depends on my experience, my upbringing, my opinion, and my point of view. It does not correspond in any way to an objective reality. All is relative.

If that is true, why are there consequences to our actions, to our words, and to our attitudes? And yes, there are consequences—consequences that are inevitable and certain.

If you should go to the top of a large bridge and jump off, it is absolutely certain what will happen. You will accelerate downwards at 9.8 meters per second per second, and you will hit the land or water. If you are not killed, you at least will be badly injured. It will happen. It is not the law of gravity that will be broken; it is you who will be broken. The law of gravity will be confirmed.

So it is with the commandments of God. We speak of breaking the commandments, but it is not the commandments that are broken. We are the ones who are broken. In our rebellion and disobedience, we only confirm the validity of the commandments. We demonstrate that they are true and right.

> You shall have no other gods before me. You shall not make for yourself an idol, nor bow down to them. You shall not

make wrongful use of the name of the LORD your God. You shall remember the Sabbath day, and keep it holy. You shall honor your father and your mother. You shall not murder. You shall not commit adultery. You shall not steal. You shall not bear false witness against your neighbor. You shall not covet anything that belongs to your neighbor (Exodus 20:1–17).

Now, if I violate one of these commandments, will God send down a lightning bolt to kill me? No, that is not the way it works, and that is not what is meant by consequences. But if I violate one of the commandments, do I undermine myself and others? Yes. Do I bring pain and hurt to myself or to my family or another person? Yes. Do I create fear and suspicion and suffering and add to the breakdown of trust in society? Yes. Are my actions destructive and detrimental? Yes. When many violate these commandments, is society thrown into a chaotic mess? Yes, yes, yes to all of the above. There are consequences to our actions, and ultimately, the consequence is death.

Faith takes seriously that God is the creator of life, the provider and Sustainer of life, the source of life. If you turn away from God, you turn away from the source of life. And if you turn away from the source of life, what is left? There is nothing left, nothing but death and the negation of all things.

Life and blessing have to do with the way we treat our neighbors, the way we treat the natural order, the way we use our time, and the way we use our money. Life and blessing depend on whether we share our bread with the hungry, whether we are forgiving, whether we are people of honesty and integrity, and whether we do justice, love kindness, and walk humbly before God (Micah 6:8).

"See, I have set before you today life and prosperity, death and adversity ... Choose life, so that you and your descendants may live, loving the LORD your God, obeying him, and holding fast to him" (Deuteronomy 30:15, 19).

There are consequences in life—consequences to be enjoyed or consequences to be suffered. That is not relative to my personal belief; it is the way it is. The choice is ours.

Moral law can be summarized very readily: "You shall love the Lord your God with all your heart, and with all your soul, and with all your strength, and with all your mind; and your neighbor as yourself" (Luke 10:27).

"Do this," Jesus said, "and you will live" (Luke 10:28).

## ❧ Why the Seventh?

"You shall not commit adultery" (Exodus 20:14).
The seventh commandment is straightforward, unbending, and easy to understand. At the same time, it seems woefully out of step with the current age, when the definition of marriage has expanded to include homosexual relationships and when it is widely assumed that what takes place between two consenting adults is their business. Is it time to revise the Ten Commandments down to nine and to recognize that the prohibition of adultery may have been suitable for a bygone age but not for our lives today?

Old fossil that I am, I would ask that we consider a few things before we totally dismiss the seventh commandment to the garbage bins of history.

The argument that consenting adults can do what they wish is clearly indefensible, as consenting adults can crash planes into buildings and plant bombs at the Boston Marathon. And while it is true that this commandment came at a time when marriage was understood to be a male/female relationship, I see no reason why the wisdom behind it does not apply to gay or lesbian relationships as well.

We need to realize that the body is not in some way evil or that sex is bad. Sexual intimacy is a wonderful, beautiful, and marvelous gift of God. Of course, like all of God's gifts, it is to be used in a loving and caring way and not in a way that is manipulative, abusive, or self-serving. In sexual intimacy, two people are united, both physically and emotionally, in a union so fulfilling that, to use the love poetry of Genesis, "a man leaves his father and his mother and clings to his wife, and they become one flesh" (Genesis 2:24). In the sexual intimacy of male and female, creatures of dust are enabled to join with God in the process of creation, a life-forming and life-giving act. Making love is a sacred thing. Enjoy it, cherish it, honor it, and give thanks to God for it.

So why does God command: no adultery?

Adultery is not a sin of sex. Adultery is a sin against the family. It is a sin that weakens and undermines the precious ties that hold a family together. It puts asunder those whom God has joined together. When a married partner becomes involved in an affair with someone else, it violates the intimate bond of the marital relationship. And even more devastating, it destroys trust in the relationship. Trust is essential in any relationship, and it is especially essential in the intimate relationship of marriage. When trust is lost, it is very difficult to hold the relationship together. Pain and suffering are the direct consequence, both for the betrayed partner and for children who may be growing up in the home. Families can be split apart and homes can be broken.

Like all of God's commandments, the one forbidding adultery is not given for God's benefit. It is given for our benefit. God can get along very well, thank you, whether we commit adultery or not. But God wants us to be fulfilled, to have relationships based on love and faithfulness, and to save and preserve our marriages. It is not a legalistic matter, grounded in some primitive law or custom. It is grounded in God's will and purpose for our lives.

The seventh commandment is not an obsolete restriction to be rejected by enlightened and freedom-loving adults. It is actually good news. It points us to a higher ground, a nobler way, and a better conduct. It shows us that we do not have to be conformed to the practices of the world around us. We are under the will and purpose of God, and we can live our lives by God's standard. And that is profoundly good news.

We are saved by love, real love, lasting love, unconditional love. We are saved by love that does not turn away and cannot be diluted, distracted, or weakened in any way. We are saved by love that is faithful and certain, caring, giving, and kind. We are saved by the love of God.

By living in that steadfast love, our marriages will be renewed, our lives will be blessed, and our homes will be dwellings of peace and concord.

## The Option

It was one of those days that was like an emotional roller coaster. One moment, we were laughing and excited and optimistic; the next, we found tears welling up in our eyes, a lump in our throats, and sorrow in our hearts. Our younger son was leaving for college. Yes, my wife and I would visit him at school, and we knew he would be home for Christmas. But an era in our lives was ending, and our home would never again be the same.

All people experience moments like that. Leaving home, changing careers, moving to a new location, getting married, retiring, a death in the family—all are times that result in a major transition in life. We close the door on one part of life and move, somewhat joyfully, somewhat fearfully, into a whole new phase of living.

When each of our sons left home, we personally experienced two sobering realities.

First, our children are not our own. Of course we commonly refer to our children as "our sons" or "our daughters." But ultimately, they are not ours. They belong to God. They are God's sons and daughters. God has created them, God has given them a unique life, and God will give them a glorious destiny. They live in our homes for a few, brief, passing years and then move on. All children are like that. They belong to God and not to us.

And the second sobering reality is that the passage of time brings change. The inescapable truth for each human being is that we are moving through time, or more accurately, rushing through time, and time brings change with it. That is a reality of life, as inevitable and as dependable as the law of gravity. Time brings change. Sometimes the change can be painful. But however painful the change may be, resistance to change may be even more painful. God forbid that we become crusty old curmudgeons who are so set in our ways that we cannot graciously accept the changes that come our way and make whatever adjustments we may need to make.

The biblical letters of Saint Peter were written at a time of significant change in the early church. Widespread persecutions took place, as early believers were tortured and sent to their deaths in cruel and horrible ways (1 Peter 4:12). False teachers promoted "destructive opinions" and "licentious ways" (2 Peter 2:1–2). Some believers lost their faith, doubtful that the promises of Christ would ever be fulfilled (2 Peter 3:8–9). In the midst of widespread change, Peter ended his correspondence with these challenging words: "But grow in the grace and knowledge of our Lord and Savior Jesus Christ. To him be the glory both now and to the day of eternity. Amen" (2 Peter 3:18).

Change is inevitable. Growth is an option. Growth is always an option. I cannot stop change from happening, but I can choose to grow in the process. I can choose to stagnate, to decline, to shrivel up. Or I can choose to expand my horizons, learn new insights, and experience new possibilities. Growth may not come easily. Growth may take work, It may take study. It may take discipline. It may take the willingness to begin a new direction. It may take risk. It may take sacrifice. But whatever it takes, I need to make the effort, pay the price, and submit to the discipline. I need to keep on growing.

It is said that an old dog cannot learn new tricks. But who wants to be an old dog? I don't want to be an old dog. I don't want to be a victim. I don't want to be a mere survivor. I want to be one of God's resurrection people who is able to move into the future with hope and confidence. The Lord "is making all things new" (Revelation 21:5). And if he is making all things new, he is making me new as well. And that is a good thing, for I have lots of growing I need to do.

O God, you are beyond time, but I am in it. The future is rushing in upon me and my world is changing fast. Open my eyes to new things that you are doing. Lead me in your way. Keep me ever open to the new possibilities that you have purposed for me.

And may I always choose the option of growth.

# It Is Good

It is good to look up at the heavens and see the stars at night. It is good to sit at the beach and look out at the vastness of the ocean. It is good to trek the mountains and gaze on spectacular and majestic peaks. It is good to experience these things.

It is good for youth, who think they are immortal and invulnerable and have no need for any power beyond themselves. It is good for the middle-aged, who must shoulder many responsibilities and challenges and who may be too distracted to recognize any power beyond themselves. It is good for the elderly, for whom declining health and the scarcity of remaining days may be an ever-present worry and who, in moments of depression, may think there is no power beyond themselves. It is good for the world's ignorant, impoverished masses, who totally depend upon a power beyond themselves. And it is good for the educated and affluent, who may falsely assume they have no need for a power beyond themselves.

At the ocean, in the mountains, and looking up at the starry host, I can be only astonished. I can stand only in awe and wonder. I am forced out of my miniscule world, out of my self-centered agenda, and out of the routine of daily life. I am moved beyond my trivialities. My perspective is changed. What seemed like a major insult becomes a little offense. What seemed like catastrophe becomes an opportunity to increase character and strength. What seemed like an overwhelming problem is reduced to a puzzle that can be solved, one piece at a time.

The ocean, the mountains, and the heavens give me depth. It is a spatial depth, as I realize that I am but a grain of sand before the ocean, a speck of dust before the mountains, and a minute particle before the stretches of the universe. But I can also experience a depth of a different order, a spiritual depth, a depth of the Spirit. And in those precious moments, I must surely comprehend the Presence of a reality beyond myself, an infinite majesty that far transcends the smallness of my control.

It is good to look up to the heavens, to behold the ocean, to gaze upon the mountains.

# Words

A chill November wind blew down upon the hills of southern Pennsylvania. Not long before, the wheat fields were gold with grain, and the peach orchards were laden with rich, ripe fruit. But now this gentle farmland would be dedicated as a cemetery, already filled with the graves of 3,500 young men. Long rows of white crosses stretched out, indistinguishable save for the names of those who lay beneath the sod.

The speaker for the day was Edward Everett, the perfect choice for such a solemn occasion. Suave and handsome, with flowing gray hair, Everett was the most famous and distinguished orator of his time. He spoke for an hour fifty-seven minutes. Bored and restless, the assembled audience dreaded the approach of yet a second speaker to the podium. How much longer would this have to go on? But there he was, a tall and homely man, standing at the podium. Silently, he removed an envelope from his pocket, on which he had written some hastily scribbled notes. He spoke but ten sentences in a span of two minutes and returned to his seat. The crowd offered a polite but perfunctory applause and then dispersed to their homes or businesses. The following day, the morning newspapers simply would write, almost in passing, that President Lincoln spoke at Gettysburg.

Two speeches were made at Gettysburg that day in 1863: one of them was just so much hot air; the other left an immortal impression upon the spirit of a war-torn nation. And that is precisely how significant, or how worthless, words can be. Words can be helpful, positive, and uplifting. And words can be harmful, deceitful, and destructive. Words accompany the most meaningful events of our lives: from "It's a boy!" or "It's a girl!" at a birth, to "With this ring I thee wed" at a marriage, to "ashes to ashes, dust to dust" at a funeral. Words make it possible to express our deepest needs and feelings, to communicate our hopes and dreams, to receive an education, to get a job, and to come to faith. Or words can be empty and meaningless, an idle chatter that is devoid of any value. Words can have the eloquence of the Twenty-Third Psalm, or words can be two old biddies sharing gossip over the back fence. Words convey the most profound thoughts of human wisdom and reveal the loving purposes of the living God. And words can be irresponsible rumors that fly from mouth to mouth. Words can be a blessing. And words can be a curse.

The Lord Jesus Christ intentionally emphasized the importance of words in a fearful warning: "I tell you, on the day of judgment you will have to give an account for every careless word you utter; for by your words you will be justified, and by your words you will be condemned" (Matthew 12:36–37).

Every careless word? I shudder to think of words I have spoken in anger; words that have brought pain to another person, even to those I deeply love; words that I dearly wish could be retracted but of course, once spoken, cannot be unuttered. I must fall on my knees and seek a merciful pardon, for it is not by my words that I shall be saved.

Environmentalists are rightly concerned about the air pollution that comes from coal-burning power plants and toxic vehicle exhaust. Surely we must also be concerned about the verbal air pollution that comes from words that are noxious and malignant.

The letter to the Ephesians tells us how to live as God's people: "Let no evil talk come out of your mouths, but only what is useful for building up, as there is need, so that your words may give grace to those who hear" (Ephesians 4:29).

What does this mean for our lives? It means that we refrain from swearing at the person who cuts us off in heavy traffic. And that we do not use the body language or the hand gesture that goes along with it. It means that we avoid all those things that weaken relationships, create ill will, and destroy community. No quarreling. No bitterness. No ruining the reputation of others. No gossip. No sniping jabs. No deceit. No verbal assaults on another person. Instead, we use words that are encouraging, kind, and loving. We are of Christ, and therefore, we use Christlike words.

You can say anything in a nice way. You can disagree agreeably. You can show respect for your opponents. You can speak the truth in love (Ephesians 4:15). With the right words, you can even love your enemies, do good to those who hate you, bless those who curse you, and pray for those who abuse you (Luke 6:27–28).

I am grateful for guards who protect from harm, whether it is the school-crossing guard, the guard at the baggage check-in at the airport, or the guard at the prison wall. I am grateful for guards who keep me from danger.

Thus, I pray for myself with the words of the psalmist: "Set a guard over my mouth, O Lord, keep watch over the door of my lips! Do not turn my heart to any evil" (Psalm 143:3, 4a).

## ✺ The Cantaloupe

In the field it lay, encrusted with dirt from a late day's summer thunderstorm, the kind where long and jagged streaks of light erupt from the darkened sky, and thundering waves of sound rattle the windows of nearby homes. But then it was picked, washed, and carefully laid on a pile with others, on a long flat table at a roadside stand. Slowly, I examined it, as a master jeweler might examine a precious gem, for indeed it was a precious thing, though it cost but two dollars. For this cantaloupe miraculously came forth from the ground, containing nutrients that, by another miraculous process, can be absorbed by my body, providing yet another miracle, life. I studied its tough skin, looking for any trace of green that announced that it was not ripe. I smelled where the stem once held it to the vine, checking for just the right aroma. I gave it a thump with my knuckle, listening for what I thought was just the proper sound. Was it ripe? Would it be a good one? I paid the girl behind the stand and took it home, and after thanking God that for one more day I have been given my daily bread, I tasted its juicy flesh and delighted in the sweetness of its flavor.

Why does it exist, this cantaloupe? I have no doubt that the wise ones are correct, that it is the product of millions of years of subtle changes, evolving from a single cell in whatever strange and mysterious processes a plant may develop. That tells me how it came to be, and for that I am grateful. But what I want to know is why it came to be. Why does it exist, this melon that emerged from a blossom in a field, flourished in the rain and sunshine, and tabled at a roadside stand?

Does it exist to be eaten? Is that the purpose of its being? Or am I a deluded and senile old fool to ask if it even has a purpose? But I am not deluded that it did come forth from the earth, that it does exist, and that I can eat it. So for me, it does have a purpose. For me and for every child of God who has ever eaten a piece of fruit, a bowl of rice, a tomato- and pepper-topped pizza pulled on a wooden paddle from an oven made of brick, fruits and vegetables and grains have a purpose—they give us life and sustenance.

Could it be that this simple melon, one of countless millions, fulfills the purpose of its existence by losing itself, and thereby giving life to others? Apart from that, it would lay rotting in the field while swarming flies surrounded its decomposing body.

Could it be that losing self is the purpose of my life, that my existence serves no purpose but self-giving? Could it be that to love the Lord your God with all your heart and soul and mind and to love your neighbor as yourself is not only a commandment but indeed the foundation on which the whole universe is established (Matthew 22:37–38)? Could it be that from the micro-seconds when the first photons burst forth upon the darkness, this whole universe has existed for no other reason than to love, and to give, and to serve and, as the Westminster Confession affirms, to glorify the Creator and to enjoy him forever?

Lord, the earth is full of your creatures; in wisdom you have made them all (Psalm 104:24).

Forgive me, oh God, when I take for granted even the most mundane of your witnesses, even those that speak without voice and praise without singing, even a cantaloupe on a roadside stand.

## The Eagle

High above the earth the eagle hovers, a majestic picture of strength and power. But it is not the eagle's strength that enables it to fly. When an eagle flies, it does not frantically flap its wings, struggling to stay aloft.

In a seemingly effortless manner, it catches uplifting drafts of wind and drifts with the currents of the air. Like a sailboat gliding across the sea under the power of the wind, the eagle ascends into the heavens by a power that is not its own.

So it is that our human strength comes from a power beyond our own finite lives. Life, health, senses, intelligence, reason, and insight all come from beyond ourselves. I find that when I rely upon my own strength, I am the weakest. I am strongest when I rely upon the resources that have no limit. In that divine and eternal might, there is a power that is healing, energizing, and life-giving.

Permit me to share a custom that has been extremely helpful for me. Perhaps it will be useful for you as well.

When I am stressed and tension-filled, I make it a point to give myself a time-out. I find a quiet place to sit, and I meditate on the words of the psalmist: "Be still, and know that I am God!" (Psalm 46:10a). I slowly repeat that verse over and over to myself: "Be still and know that I am God! Be still and know that I am God! Be still and know that I am God!" I begin to see things in a new and greater perspective. Struggles and challenges lose their grip upon me. The time crunch that was so compelling is replaced with a quiet assurance that there will be time; there will be time. The tension slips away, and the stress subsides. Peace is restored.

God is not like me, a finite human who can choose to love or not to love. God is love (1 John 4:8). Love is at the center of God's nature. And God does not stop loving. God knows me in all my needs and loves me anyway. God's love is sufficient for all my needs.

When Israel was captive in exile, a great spokesperson for the Lord gave words of encouragement: "Those who wait for the Lord shall renew their strength, they shall mount up wings like eagles, they shall run and not be weary, they shall walk and not faint" (Isaiah 40:31).

Stop your frantic flapping. Rely on an infinite source of strength and goodness.

Soar like an eagle.

# Roots

Man's best friend is a … tree! Oh, I know the correct answer is a dog, but trees must surely be high on the list of best friends. Trees provide shade, fruits and nuts, wood for our homes and furniture, paper and cardboard, pencils, and toothpicks. Trees act as filters to clean the air and water, and they store huge quantities of carbon to reduce the effects of global warming. And trees are beautiful. They have trunks that are tall and erect, soaring toward the heavens; branches that stretch out in every direction in a magnificent canopy; and leaves that are rich and verdant in the dark green of summer or the myriad colors of the fall. What a wonderful blessing. What a wonderful gift of God are trees.

When we look at a tree, we only see part of it. What we cannot see is a vast network of roots under the ground. Those roots spread out as wide as the crown of the tree is wide. In some species, two-thirds of the tree is the roots. They extend deep into the earth, reaching out to an aquifer of life-giving water. Without the roots, the tree would topple over in the first strong wind that blows. Without roots, the tree would shrivel and die from the lack of moisture and nutrients. As the tree grows, the roots also grow. Actually, it is the other way around. It is the growth of the root system that enables the tree to grow. If the roots fail to grow, the tree will stagnate and be stunted.

Six centuries before the birth of Christ, the prophet Jeremiah made a striking contrast between two very different images (Jeremiah 17:5–8). One image is of a tree, planted by water. The tree thrives and flourishes. Its roots are enriched by the stream. It does not cease to bear fruit. Its leaves remain green, even in the time of drought. The other image is a shrub in the desert. It struggles to survive. In the desolate and barren sand, it may shoot up in the spring, clinging desperately to the ground. With the scorching heat of the summer, it will wither and die. It is not a casual comparison. It is the difference between growth and stagnation, between flourishing and withering, and between life and death. And it all depends on the roots, whether the tree is rooted in a source of life or rooted in desert sand.

Jeremiah is not just talking about trees, is he? He is speaking about human life. In the historic context, he is talking about Judah of the early sixth century BC, a people who abandoned faith in the God of Abraham, Isaac, and Jacob. False gods were pursued, commandments were ignored and broken, and injustice was rampant in the land. People lived in the complacent assumption that faithlessness had no consequences. That naive way of life would radically end when the Babylonian army invaded the land, destroyed Jerusalem, and marched its citizens into exile. Of these people, Jeremiah said: "Cursed are those who trust in mere mortals and make mere flesh their strength, whose hearts turn away from the Lord … All who forsake you shall be put to shame; those who turn away from you shall be recorded in the underworld, for they have forsaken the fountain of living water, the Lord" (Jeremiah 17:5, 13).

Jeremiah is not just talking about people long ago, is he? He is speaking to our world, our time in history, our lives. The daily hustle and bustle, rushing from one place to the next, chattering nonstop on our cell phones or mindlessly playing games on our electronic toys, growing restless in traffic jams, worrying incessantly about money, trying at all cost to advance our careers or accumulate more wealth, maintaining our homes and lawns and boats and cars—these are the branches of our lives. This is what we see, what we judge, what we envy, what we look for. And Jeremiah says, don't look to these things. Look to the roots, where life is preserved, sustained, enriched, and fulfilled.

Look not to the branches but to the roots. Are you rooted in the source of life, or are you rooted in dry and withering sand? Are you rooted in an infinite source of love and strength? Are you rooted in the One at whose word the universe was thrown into being, the One who owns the cattle on a thousand hills (Psalm 50:10), the One who calls forth the heavenly host by name and not one of them is missing (Isaiah 40:26)? Are you rooted in the One whose faithfulness is revealed from generation to generation and whose steadfast love shall last forever (Psalm 100:5)? Are you rooted in him who broke out from the tomb and who has conquered the power of death (Revelation 1:18)? He proclaims to the world: "I am the resurrection and the life. Those who believe in me, even though they die, will live, and everyone who lives and believes in me will never die" (John 11:25–26).

Where are your roots? Indeed, do you even have them?

# Patrick

He came to a land where steep and rocky cliffs are battered by the crashing waves of an often turbulent sea. Green—yes, countless shades of green—adorns this land year-round, green broken by golden outbursts of thorny gorse, the wisps of smoke from peat-burning fires in scattered gray-stone habitations, and the soft white coats of sheep grazing in the fields. It is a land where spectacular scenery and raw, harsh struggles to survive have been strangely intermingled. Occasionally, an entire day is warmed by direct sunlight; most of the time, the weather reports speak of "mist and murk" or describe conditions that are "rainy" or "blowy."

The man who came to this land was a son of privilege and comfort. Raised in a Roman home in the fifth century AD, he was educated in both classical thought and in sacred Scripture. As a teenager, he was captured by slave traders, transported in bondage across the Irish Sea, and forced to work as a shepherd in a remote, stone-covered hillside known as Slemish. He was cold, hungry, and alone most of the time, often wet and miserable. Yet he prayed day and night, as many a hundred prayers a day, as he later recorded.

One day, he heard a voice: "Your ship is waiting." He took that as a sign to run away, and he fled. He walked some two hundred miles to the coast near Wexford, where, sure enough, a ship was about to sail. Somehow, he bartered with the captain for passage and eventually found his way back home.

But this home, like all earthly homes, was only temporary. Again, a voice came to him, this time "the voice of the Irish," begging him to return. Return he did, to shepherd a human flock and convert thousands to the faith. And here was his method of success: he came with love and humility—never resentful, never self-righteous—allowing those who heard his witness to keep their customs and traditions. Using a common shamrock as an image, he proclaimed not despising condemnation but good news: the God you worship when the sun rises on the winter solstice is a Father, a brother, a constant presence; one God who offers the gift of eternal life. He preached, taught, and developed communities of followers. These became the early Irish monks who, transcribing letter by letter in cold, stone-walled cells, copied sacred texts and classic works, and thus preserved both faith and civilization in those Dark Ages after the fall of Rome.*

Several old traditions surround this man. He drove away the snakes. No, not literal snakes, of course, but the snakes of ignorance and superstition were removed by his influence. Early one morning, before first light, an Irish king looked out from his seat of power on the hill of Tara. On a distant hillside, he saw a large fire burning. He summoned his chieftains and told them, "Unless we extinguish that fire, it will consume us." His prophecy was accurate, for the fire was a Pascal fire, lit to greet the Easter dawn and celebrate the resurrection of the Christ. That fire, set by the man who was once a slave, did consume the land, not with violence and force but with gentleness, hope, and love.

The name of this man was Patrick, now preceded with the highest of earthly accolades, "Saint." When the frosty landscape of mid-March gives way to a sun-warmed, flowered spring, lift a cold, dark Smithwick's, Harp, or Guinness in his honor. And lift a prayer of thanks to the shamrock-like God whose saving love embraces not only the sons of privilege but the frugal people of a rocky coastland, living on a distant, windswept shore.

---

\*   The far-reaching significance of the Irish monks is brilliantly described by Thomas Cahill in *How the Irish Saved Civilization*, a volume well worth the reading.

# ✣ The Garden

I have never seen a garden where only flowers grow. No matter how lush and fragrant are the blossoms of iris, foxglove, or marigold, weeds always grow beside them.

Philosophically, I cannot account for this. Why should there not be a garden where only flowers grow? Why not a universe where there is only good, not evil? I do not know the answer. Perhaps, in the realities of this world, it has to be the way it is. In this world, the sun shines and the raindrops fall where they will, and the nutrient-rich soil receives any seeds, however intentionally or accidentally they may be sown. The Creator, who grants free will to His sons and daughters, has engineered a world where microscopic cells have the capacity to evolve into calla lilies or into ragweed, into higher life-forms or into malignancies. The gift of freedom, be it human free choice or universal free process, does not ensure that all choices are good or that all happenings are fortuitous.

I cannot comprehend the mysteries of good and evil. I must trust that the One who has fashioned the creation has also opened the possibility of a new creation. The Lord of life has promised resurrection to a realm where all wrongs will one day be made right, and I lay claim to that promise.

What I can discern is this: what is true of the garden is true of life.

In every neighbor I may see a destructive perversity that lurks deep within the soul, or I may see a noble saintliness that may shine forth.

In any mealtime, there is the chance to wolf down my food, complain about the problems of the day, or lose all self-composure when my two-year old throws his vegetables on the floor. Or I can see that mealtime is a sacred moment, an opportunity to lift a prayer of thanks for this, my daily bread, and to connect with family and friends in the intimate and fundamental experience of sharing a meal together.

And at any given moment, I can smell the noxious exhaust of an engine, or I can breathe deeply of pine and spruce. I can hear the dull noise of an overcrowded highway, or I can delight in the sound of the jay. I can open my eyes and look around me to see littered debris in the meadow, potholes in the roadway, and dark clouds on the hilltop. Or I can see the play of sunlight in the forest leaves. I can look upon the lilacs, or I can gaze upon the weeds.

For there is no garden where only flowers grow.

##  The River

The great river of time moves unceasingly from the past, through the present, and on to the future.

I stand on the bank of the river and look out at the span of my life. Sometimes flowing peacefully and sometimes surging and raging, that small part of the river includes some incredibly significant events: the end of World War II and the collapse of the Soviet Union; the use of nuclear energy, from weapons of mass destruction to power plants; a vaccine for polio and the massive development of antibiotics; Brown vs. the Board of Education, and the Civil Rights Act; landing a human on the moon; the transition from slide rules and mechanical calculators to a world where a handheld phone can surf the Internet, take digital photos, and send text messages to a friend; and the mapping of the three billion chemical pairings that compose the human genome. That small part of the river also includes countless mundane and ordinary events (as if any moment is anything but miraculous and extraordinary): sunrises and sunsets; bowls of cereal and cups of coffee; miles of driving on superhighways and back roads; times of study, from learning that "Jesus Loves Me" to reading Patristic Christology in the Greek texts; hearing the cry of a blue jay or the crash of an ocean wave upon the shore; and sharing with family in moments that seem so common but are precious beyond any measure.

I stand on the bank of the river and look back to the past. I am limited by what I can see, for the further back I look, the more my view is restricted by the bends of the river, the shortness of sight, and the settling of the evening fog. Yet there are tools that help me see far back into the past: written histories, archeological discoveries, museums, even computer-generated pictures from the Hubble telescope that reveal a time approaching the first dawning of light in this universe.

I stand on the bank and look out to the future. I know not what a day may bring forth, as an old prayer tells us, but to some small extent I can imagine where the river might be headed—continuing conflict in world geo-politics, continuing scientific advances, the discovery of some form of life on other planets, cars that drive themselves, increasing population, challenges from the refusal to limit consumption of fossil fuels, more tragedy from the mindless insistence that anyone, no matter how young, how troubled, or how deranged has a right to own a gun. I look to a personal future, and I foresee declining abilities and to the time when, like all the flowers of the field, I shall be no more.

I stand on the bank and look and wonder and pray.

But in reality, no one stands on the bank. We are not by the river but in the river. The events of the past swirl around us, the conditions of the present immerse us, and the unstoppable course of the river carries us forward. No one is merely an objective observer; all are shaped and influenced by what has happened, is happening, and will happen; all are part of the ceaseless flow; all are moving to a future.

Holy Scripture must be read and understood in this manner. Both religious and nonreligious people miss a greater reality if they think biblical study means knowing the names of the disciples or that the Assyrians conquered the Northern Kingdom in 721 BC. Yes, those objective facts are good to know and are part of being a cultured person. But we err if we fail to understand that sacred history is *pro nobis*, for us. It is our history, our story, our lives, our failures, our hope, our salvation. We are in the river. The mighty acts of God swirl around us, the Father can be experienced and loved in the present moment, and everyone and everything is moving to a greater sea, when the Almighty will be all in all.

# ❀ First Diversion

Diversions are a normal part of life: the side trail that ventures down a narrow path on a long hike; the highway detour that forces you to alter your well-planned route; the interruption that delays or possibly cancels your carefully scheduled agenda. Diversions may bring joys that would never have been anticipated. An irritating construction project may lead you through a pleasant valley, past an orchard blossoming in springtime grandeur or to the crest of a hill where, far below, a river meanders silently through fields and pastures. Diversions may be life-changing: the book, lecture, or mission trip that calls for a new direction; the corporate or military assignment that requires leaving behind friends and established routines to form a new life in another state or country; the death of a loved one that radically changes not just a few passing weeks but leaves a lasting impact on every part of your existence and every day of the remaining life that may be granted to you. But however large or small, however gratifying or distressing, diversions are a frequent part of life in this ever-changing world.

Thus these simple offerings also have diversions, for offerings are the contributions of an offering-giver. And in these diversions, I seek to place my life, a time-bound creature miraculously graced to be a child of God, in a particular time and place in the great span of human history.

On March 1, 1945, as her soon-to-be-two-years-old son played in a carefree manner on the living room floor, a young woman received a telegram. It contained a message that every spouse of every soldier, sailor, and airman dreaded to receive. "The Secretary of War desires me to express his deep regrets that your husband, Staff Sergeant Byron V. Brought has been reported missing in action since 7 February over Austria." Byron and his nine colleagues, on a heavy bomber known as a B-24 Liberator, had been shot down on a mission to destroy a synthetic oil refinery in Moosbierbaum, twenty-two miles northwest of Vienna, Austria.

Miriam Jane Raffensperger Brought had been raised in Harrisburg, Pennsylvania, the daughter of Paul Edwin and Golda Webb Raffensperger.

Her parents came from small country towns in Adams County, not far from the Gettysburg wheat field and peach orchard where, eighty-two years earlier, the bloodiest battle ever fought in the Western Hemisphere had taken place. Paul supervised the procurement and distribution of supplies for the Pennsylvania State Department of Transportation, a demanding position, as the state was pioneering the construction of a turnpike, a modern highway that would span rivers and tunnel through mountains from Philadelphia to the Ohio border west of Pittsburgh. Golda, like virtually all women of her generation, was a homemaker. Her chores included laundering clothing with a tub and washboard, darning socks, canning tomatoes and peaches, making soap from lard and lye, and carrying bags of groceries eight city blocks from the market house. Like all good housewives, she regularly swept the steps and sidewalks in front of their row house.

Byron also was raised in Harrisburg, in a family that struggled mightily during the Great Depression. His father, Byron Vance Sr., lost his job as a switchman with the Reading Railroad and far too often found consolation by drinking heavily. Baskets of food from the local Congregational church and farm-raised produce from relatives kept the family going. The youngest of five children, Byron was only twelve when his mother, Anna Book Brought, died of cancer. The family broke apart, and Byron was sent to the Hershey Industrial School, now known as the Milton Hershey School.

Jane (so called as she never went by her first name) met Byron while he was working as a salesman in Doutrich's, a men's clothing store, and she was employed wrapping gift packages in Pomeroy's Department Store. For years, the family joked about the way they met. Gift wrapping was a service provided free of charge to customers, but Byron first approached Jane with the line, "If you charge a quarter for the next packages you wrap, we would have enough money to go the movies. But even if you don't, I would like you to go to the movies with me."

The mission over Moosbierbaum on that February 7 was fraught with danger. Following the Normandy landing in June 1944, Allied armies made slow but steady progress pushing the Germans back toward their homeland. But by the end of the year, German divisions made a strong counteroffensive. In the east, the advance of the Red Army had been stalled, with enormous loss of life on both sides. And the December Nazi offensive in the Ardennes (the Battle of the Bulge) resulted in nearly ninety thousand American casualties—killed, wounded, or taken prisoner. Fighting was intense on the land and in the air. Continuous bombing, American by day and British by night, was taking a devastating toll on German industrial production, especially on the refining of gasoline. General Eisenhower later noted the importance of destroying the German refineries:

"Her [German] troops in every sector were constantly embarrassed by lack of fuel for vehicles. The effect was also felt by the Luftwaffe, in which training of new pilots had to be sharply curtailed because of fuel shortages" (*Crusade in Europe*, page 368).

A groan and audible curses went up from the assembled crews as they gathered for a predawn briefing of their daily mission on February 7. Hitler knew that he had to protect his remaining refineries, and as a result, Moosbierbaum was heavily defended with one hundred anti-aircraft guns. Intense flak had caused severe losses in two previous attempts to destroy the refinery. This was not to be a "milk run," as missions to lightly fortified targets was known, but an extremely dangerous attack in which planes and crews would surely be lost. It was a maximum effort with the entire wing participating, accompanied by twenty black-and-yellow checkered-tailed P-51 Mustangs, piloted by African American pilots. Take off was at 0800; target time 1236.

Weather was always a flight hazard for bombing crews in World War II. Forecasts were often inadequate, due to the lack of well-positioned reporting stations. Cloud-covered targets resulted in inaccurate bombing, and weather changes in route led to occasional turn-backs. Temperatures on board the planes dropped to that of a frigid Arctic landscape. Like all turret gunners, Byron carried an extra oxygen mask for use when the one he was wearing froze up from his exhaled breath.

The flak was solid as they turned on the bomb run, eight bursts across, to the left and to the right. Thirty seconds before target, a shell exploded close to engine number 4, creating a huge black trail from hot vaporizing oil. Just after "Bombs away," the piercing sound of metal crashing through metal meant the plane had taken a direct hit, knocking out engines number 2 and number 4 and severing the gas line to engine number 1. Losing altitude, pilot Joe Ballinger could no longer hold formation, and the crew began jettisoning everything that could be pried loose. Within ten minutes, the plane lost 17,000 feet of altitude. Engine number 1 went out, and Joe called out the fearful order to prepare for a crash. The plane came down on a plowed, snow-covered corn field, several hundred yards south of the Cazma River. German soldiers were on the north. Upon impact, the left front wheel snapped off, and the plane slid along the ground on its belly, headed for a cluster of houses. The pilot slammed left rudders and aileron; the plane jerked 180 degrees to the left and came to a stop. Miraculously, no one was hurt and fire did not erupt. Two P-51s that had followed them down tipped their wings, a reassuring sign that their position was known and would be reported.

Quickly, the crew destroyed the Norden bombsight, a high-tech instrument of its day, to keep it from falling into German hands. A group of partisans arrived and offered assistance. After removing first-aid and ration kits from the plane, the partisans took them to a farmhouse near Stefanje, where they were fed and sheltered. Remarkably, one of the partisans, Ivan Antonocich, had lived in McKeesport, Pennsylvania, and spoke English. On Valentine's Day, a Halifax bomber dropped canned goods and supplies. A downed British crew met up with them in Grabovnia, Croatia, and ironically, on March 1, the day the telegram arrived, a South African Air Force C-47 landed and took them out.

Back in Harrisburg, on that fateful day when the telegram arrived, the news spread quickly. "Missing in Action" meant one of two things: either the crew had been killed or had been captured. Neighbors and friends came to the house to share their concern. The town newspaper reported: "Staff Sgt. Byron Brought Lost in Austrian Mission." Although Jane was a faithful Methodist, the local Catholic church held a special mass. That night, a fearful and anxious Jane turned to her Bible. Before Byron had left for military duty, he and Jane had agreed to read the same chapter of the Bible each night. It was a way of staying connected with God and with one another while they were apart. The reading that night was the twenty-seventh chapter of Acts, a passage in which Saint Paul and his companions survived a shipwreck. The last verse of the chapter, verse 44, reads: "And so it was that all were brought safely to land."

All were brought safely to land! Jane read those words and received them as a sign from God that Byron and his entire crew were safe and alive. A woman of unflinching faith, she believed that good news. Not until several weeks later did she learn that indeed her husband and the crew were all alive.

The love between Jane and Byron remained strong until their deaths, five days apart in January 2002, after sixty years of marriage. It was an unconditional love. There were arguments, some heated, and there were difficult times, but the love prevailed, for richer or poorer, in sickness and in health, for better or for worse.

There is no greater blessing in this life than to live in a family with unconditional love. I never had to learn about unconditional love from a textbook—I saw it, I received it, and I experienced it from my parents.

For I was that toddler playing on the living room floor in March 1945. And I am incredibly grateful that Jane and Byron were known to me as Mom and Dad.

# A Projection?

It is time for you to come of age, they tell me, to become mature, to enter the modern, scientific world, and to relinquish the outdated and superstitious thinking of the past. There is no Supreme Being, no God, no Creator. The universe consists of matter and energy, nothing more. Everything is reducible to mechanistic forces and reactions that science can explain—or one day will explain—eliminating the naïve need for an imagined divine. What you call "God" is only an illusion, the outward projection of an infantile need for security and well-being. The need is there, so you project, from your own human nature, a supernatural, powerful, and benevolent Being who will love you, protect you, and care for your needs, not only in this world but in a projected world to come.

I readily concede that I am insecure. No matter how much money is in my bank account, no matter how many assets I may accumulate, no matter how may vitamins I may take each day, no matter how carefully I may regulate my diet, no matter that I wear a seatbelt and refuse to drive under the influence, and no matter what I may do or not do, I am going to die. I know that. It is not a matter of speculation. And as if an awareness of a certain death is not enough, in this world I constantly live under the threat of illness and personal decline, ever endangered by the fury of the elements or the violence of other people, continually fearful of adversity for family and friends.

And so I, along with religious people in every time and place, project a big daddy in the sky to provide reassurance, so that I may rest content in delusional peace and comfort.

But if this were true, if God is a projection of my wishes, I would not have projected the God who is God. My projected God would be much more convenient and much less demanding. The God of my projection would readily allow me to remain lustful, greedy, self-centered, resentful, petty, and envious.

One day, a rich young man came to Jesus and asked that fundamental question of all the children of the dust: "What must I do to inherit eternal life?" Jesus answered, "Sell all that you have and give it to the poor, and follow me" (Luke 18:18–25). Sell everything? Give up all your earthly securities? I don't think I would have projected a God like that.

I would not project a God who commands me to love my enemies (Matthew 5:44). No merely human person in his right mind would do that. I would not project a God who commands me not to worry about my body, about what I will eat, or what I will drink, or what I will put on (Matthew 6:25). Those concerns are part of my daily life. I would not project a God who commands (not suggests, but *commands*): "If anyone strikes you on the right cheek, turn the other also" (Matthew 5:38). What idiot would do that? And I definitely would not project a God who requires me to deny myself and take up a cross (Luke 9:23). Taking up a cross is not on my top ten list of things I would like to do.

A projection?

If God is a human projection, the projection would be irrational and unexplainable from a human point of view, ludicrous to the point of being comical, and a very strange projection indeed.

# The Fool

There is a chapter in the Bible that is repeated two times. Other than a few minor word differences, Psalm 14 and Psalm 53 are identical. Why would a psalm be repeated? Is it a mistake of the publisher? Was some ancient scribe asleep at the switch? Was the psalmist a declining Alzheimer's patient who would tell a story, enjoy a good laugh, and then ten minutes later repeat the same story? None of the above is the probable answer. The most likely explanation is that the old rabbis who canonized the Hebrew Scripture were quite intentional in including the passage in two locations. Apparently, the text has something terribly important to teach us.

The opening verse of both psalms is a striking attack on atheism: "The fool says in his heart 'there is no God.'" Those who deny the existence of God and those who go about their lives as if there is no God are fools. The verse does not say that nonbelievers are evil or wicked people; indeed, they may be very nice persons—decent and law-abiding citizens, helpful to others, the sort of folks with whom you would enjoy a friendly chat over a cold beer or a cup of gourmet coffee. But nonetheless, they are fools. Their false assumption results in a profound misunderstanding of reality. Atheists just don't get it.

Underlying all atheism is nihilism.

Apart from God, death reigns supreme. Despite all human accomplishments; all reasoned scientific explanations; all magnificent painting, sculpture, and music; and all achievements of the world's greatest cultures, without God, death has the final word. Despite all the medical advances, all the advanced pharmaceuticals, all the brilliant surgical techniques, and all the remarkable technology common in any intensive care unit, all who live and breathe will die. Despite all the memorials, all the kind words spoken at "Celebration of Life" observances, and all the forms of ancestor worship, make no mistake: death will have dominion. All living creatures, great and small, will die. To pretend otherwise is to play the fool.

Apart from God, injustice goes unanswered. What justice can there be for victims of the Holocaust, for children who have died of starvation, for the teenager gunned down on the streets of any American city, or for the woman who happens to be buying vegetables in a middle Eastern market at the exact time a suicidal fanatic detonates his explosive vest? Without God to ultimately make things right, the hope that good will triumph over evil is a naïve illusion. Indeed, without God, all hope is short-lived and meets with inevitable frustration, like a cancer patient whose life may be extended a few passing weeks by a drastic medical intervention but who then dies. To pretend otherwise is to play the fool.

Apart from God, there is no meaning and no purpose to life. What meaning can there be in a universe that will pass away and come to nothing? What purpose can there be for one who is taken from the dust of the earth and will return to the dust of the earth once again? To presume meaning and purpose apart from God is to play the fool.

Apart from God, love has no greater reality than a passing emotion that will quickly fade and be no more. Like impassioned lovers who find themselves in the divorce court in a few brief years, love will have no lasting significance, no redeeming quality, and no power to ultimately make a difference. It, too, will be obliterated by death. To pretend otherwise is to play the fool.

Apart-from-God ethics make no sense. If there is no God, why not have a Holocaust? Your people are coming out of a worldwide depression. Your people were humiliated and impoverished in a previous war. Your people need *lebensraum* (living space). The Poles have *lebensraum*. Take it from them. Your people need wealth. The Jews have wealth. Take it from them. Take their money, their bonds, their securities, their shops, their homes, and yes, take even the gold from their teeth. Why not? Apart from God, it only makes good sense. To pretend otherwise is to play the fool.

Take away God, and nihilism is all that is left.

In momentary comfort, I read the opening verse of the psalm and congratulate myself. I believe in God. I am not a fool. These words must be addressed to someone else.

Suddenly, my complacency is taken away as I read the next few verses: "There is none that does good … They have all fallen away; they are all alike depraved." All have fallen away? All alike are depraved? Surely not me. Yes, me too. "There is none that does good, no, not one."

I sadly admit the words are true. There have been times in my life when I have thought and spoken and acted as if there were no God. I shudder to think of angry words that have passed from my lips that have been hurtful, words that I spoke as if God did not exist. I shudder to remember attitudes I have held, attitudes that were unloving and scornful, attitudes as if God did not exist. I shudder to think of deeds that I have done and of all the good that I have failed to do, deeds done and deeds neglected, as if God did not exist.

I am the fool.

God is Lord, the beginning and the end of all things, the giver of grace, and the only source of hope and life.

To rely on anything less than that is to be a fool.

## ❂ Just Take No for an Answer

It is not easy to take no for an answer. There are times when it is extremely difficult, seemingly impossible. That is especially true when no is the answer to prayer.

How do you keep faith when you hear the awful diagnosis of cancer, or when your spouse or child dies, or when the company you have worked for twenty years goes belly-up and you are laid off—and oh, by the way, you've just lost your insurance and pension as well? You pray intensely to a loving God, but silence is the only answer, the silence of an undermining and faith-shattering no.

Sickness and suffering, tragedy and death take place, crushing our hopes, destroying our dreams, and dreadfully changing our lives. It happens to the good as well as to the evil. It can happen without warning or with time to prepare. It can be painful, defeating, and devastating, and it cannot be explained. It happens. It is the way of the world.

You just have to take no for an answer.

Prayer is not a transaction, like going into a store, paying your money, and walking out with the item you desire. Prayer is a relationship. In any request, the answer may be yes, or it may be no. And so it is when the request is made to God.

In one of the churches I served, a woman learned that her husband was dying of cancer. She was a faithful woman. She attended worship regularly, prayed sincerely, and read her Bible. She prayed and prayed that her husband would be healed. There was only silence, the silence of God. Her husband died. The woman lost faith, stopped attending worship, and stopped praying. She was hurt and embittered.

One day, perhaps six months later, the woman came into my office. Her attitude had completely changed. "I now realize that God answered my prayer," she told me. "God healed my husband. It was not the healing I wanted but an ultimate healing, a healing to a realm where there is no pain and suffering." She came back to worship and resumed her life of prayer. God's no may lead to a different kind of yes.

Saint Paul wrestles with the problem of suffering in the letter to the Romans. He is troubled by the destructive and devastating realities in life, conditions that can cut you off from any sense of meaning, purpose, or well-being. Paul has a long list: "hardship, distress, persecution, famine, nakedness, peril, or sword" (Romans 8:35). These are things that can cut you off from God.

In that context of suffering, Paul says, "Wait a minute!" (He does not say that in the text, but that is what he is thinking.) He asks a question: Will anything be able to separate us from the love of Christ? (Romans 8:35).

Paul's answer is no. Actually, no is not his answer. His answer is *no!* It is not a wimpy no or a casual no; it is not the no you might answer if the waitress asks if you would like another cup of coffee, and you say,

"No, thank you." It is a clear and definite and absolute *no!* It is the *no* you say when your two-year-old is reaching out to touch the hot stove or starting to cross the street unattended. There is no question about this *no*. "I am convinced that neither death, nor life, nor angels, nor rulers, nor things present, nor things to come, nor powers, nor height, nor depth, nor anything in all creation, will be able to separate us from the love of God in Christ Jesus our Lord" (Romans 8:38–39).

Do our misfortunes mean that there is no God? *No!* That is not a logical conclusion. Does our suffering mean that God has abandoned us? *No!* That would be a false assumption. Is there anything that can destroy God's ultimate purpose for our lives? *No!* Our destiny is safe and secure. "If God is for us, who is against us?" (Romans 8:31b).

Can anything separate us from God's love?

*No! No! No!*

Just take *no* for an answer.

## ❁ Choose

Like belief in God, atheism is an act of faith. Even the greatest of theologians have failed to produce a proof of God's existence that is so convincing and unassailable that it has been universally accepted. Likewise, the most erudite of atheists have been unable to prove that there is no God. While many atheists would be hard-pressed to admit it, their position is based on faith.

Perhaps God likes it that way. God desires that his children accept a relationship that is grounded in trust and love, rather than being compelled to submit by the irresistible force of an undeniable proof. Thomas believed because he saw, but those who are blessed are those who have not seen and yet believe (John 20:29).

For believers in God, faith is more than an intellectual assent, more than simply saying, "I believe that there is a supreme reality out there somewhere." Faith is a reliance, a confidence, and a faithfulness. It involves basing your life, your attitude, your words, and your actions on the certain conviction that there is a God, that there is meaning and purpose in the universe, that God demands justice and righteousness in human life, and that ultimately, good will prevail over evil.

Faith is not an issue for agnostics. The agnostic says, "It may be that there is a God, or maybe there is not. I just don't know." Admittedly, there is something admirable about the admission of ignorance. But when we contemplate the existence of God, we are dealing with the ultimate questions of life. Does God exist? Is there purpose to my life? Is goodness the will of the divine or simply a relative value that each culture defines for itself? Is there life beyond this earthly existence? Are homo sapiens more than flesh and blood, more than physical properties? Is love a reality or a feeling? These are the issues that really matter. And when you deal with the issues that really matter, you cannot sit on the fence.

If someone asks, "Do you want corn flakes or raisin bran?" you can reasonably answer, "I don't know. It doesn't matter. I am satisfied with either." But with the ultimate issues of life, you cannot pretend that a decision is not required. You must choose, one way or the other.

It is not a matter of "Do you believe?" It is only a matter of "What do you believe?"

It is not a question of "Do you serve the Lord?" It is only a question of "Which lord do you serve?"

## How Sad

In this world there is much sadness and misfortune. Enough sadness comes from beyond our control so that we certainly need not do or say anything that brings sadness to another person. His or her sadness is quite sufficient without our adding to it. And it would be wholly irrational to increase the sadness that we ourselves may need to bear.

How sad to be obsessed with our own wants and agendas, when so often they are petty and trivial.

How sad to clutter our lives with things, when all things will break, wear out, or become obsolete.

How sad to speak about God, when, by incredible grace, I have the privilege of speaking with God.

How sad to fall asleep at the end of each day without saying, "Thank you."

How sad to stand at the graveside of a dear friend and to celebrate his/her life, without acknowledging the One who gave that life and to whom it has returned.

How sad to pout and sulk, when, with a word of forgiveness, we could have a party.

How sad to go the mall on Thanksgiving Day to save 20 percent on the current fashion or the latest electronic model, when I could share with family and friends around a festive table. Or if no family and friends are available, to serve a meal in a homeless shelter so that those with nearly nothing would have occasion to give thanks.

How sad to watch a game on the flat screen when I could play a game with my children or grandchildren in the backyard.

How sad to ever say, "If only …"

How sad to say with Thomas, "Unless it is proven to my satisfaction, I will not believe" (John 20:25).

How sad to have eyes that fail to see the golden leaves of autumn, ears that do not hear the rippling of a mountain stream, a mind that thinks it knows it all, and a heart that does not love.

How very sad indeed.

# The Question

How can there be a God when we live in world where children starve to death? How can there be a God when children perish from malaria and typhoid, are abused and molested, and suffer and die from bullets and bombs and toxic gas?

It is an age-old question, a question troubling to believers of every faith, who understand their God to be both all-powerful and all-compassionate. For anti-theists, not content to rest with their personal denial of God until faith has been destroyed in everyone, it is the ace up the sleeve, the decisive argument that they are convinced will demonstrate the proof of their arrogant delusion: there is no God. For no good God could tolerate such a condition.

In this world, children are hungry and malnourished. They lie on mats, too weak to lift their heads. Their pathetic little bodies, with swollen tummies and skinny limbs, cry out for even a cup of milk or a bowl of rice. It is true; it is real; it is now. The horrid, hideous, unacceptable reality is that children starve to death.

It is not because God does not care.

It is because we do not care.

# An Open Letter to People of Faith

Dear brothers and sisters,

I write to you as one who walks beside you in the journey of faith. Like you, I pass briefly through this world. Like you, I believe in an Almighty and transcendent reality.

I do not care what you call this great power or in what language you may speak of that which is beyond.

I do not mind that you wear a shawl and cap while standing beside an ancient wall, for I, too, feel the need to pray.

I do not mind that you kneel and press your forehead to the ground, for I, too, give myself in submission.

I do not mind that you wash in the waters of the Ganges, for I, too, need to be cleansed.

I do not mind that you sit cross-legged in deep meditation, for I, too, must find release from a life centered on myself.

I do not care about how you may express your devotion. You may assemble to hear laws written on a parchment scroll. I, too, must heed and obey those commandments. You may march around a black stone and throw pebbles at a pillar. I, too, must be delivered from evil. You may process in a festive celebration, carrying on your shoulders the representation of a large elephant head. I, too, believe that the divine is made manifest in earthly forms, and I, too, must respond in joyful celebration. It matters not whether you worship in a cathedral with breathtaking stained glass and magnificent paintings, icons, and murals, or whether you worship in a plain hall with chalk-colored walls, free of all adornment. A divine presence may be experienced in both settings.

I acknowledge that we have different religious opinions and understandings. Of course there will be differences. No two people are exactly alike, and we live with different customs and traditions. We emerge from different backgrounds and cultures. I painfully confess that our differences have led to violence and bloodshed and that our past is marred by conflict, war, and shameful atrocities. Surely this must be a deep regret to all of us.

But must our differences divide us when we have so much in common? Must our future be ruined by the sins of the past? My wife and I are unique and different persons. We both are strong-willed, and that has resulted in dissension and argument. But we have much in common. And more than that, we commit ourselves to one another in unconditional love.

Love and justice are not human constructs. They are not imagined or made up. They are not emotions that can quickly change and disappear. Both love and justice come from beyond our finite lives. They are derived from a love and justice that exists above all that is merely human. They are characteristics of that purposeful reality who has brought into being all that is or ever will be. They are given to us, and they are demanded of us. They alone are the path to peace.

Brothers and sisters, hear the cry of my heart. Let there be no more hatred, no more intolerance, and no more resentment. Let us live together in love, work together for justice, and encourage and support each other in faith. For the sake of every starving child, for the sake of every disease-ridden person, for the sake of every lonely and despairing soul, and for the sake of every lost traveler in this passing world, we must do it. For the sake of world peace, we must do it, for there will be no peace unless the people of faith can model the way. For the sake of that reality whom we commonly confess to be the Lord of the universe, we must do it.

Brothers and sisters, we must do it, and we must do it now.

# An Open Letter to All Who Do Not Believe in God

Like two peoples separated by a wide ocean, a great width divides us. It may seem that the distance cannot be overcome, for one either believes in a supreme reality, or one does not. I write to you in the hope, uncertain as it may be, that the dividing ocean between us may be crossed, and that ships bearing the trade of love and mutual support may venture freely between our shores.

Even as there are many differences among believers, so there are many differences among nonbelievers. I realize that my target audience is very diverse. Some have come to a position of atheism after careful consideration, believing that science or logic has conclusively dismissed any need for a higher power. Some have never given the matter serious thought, so preoccupied are they with their own agendas that the question of God simply has not crossed their minds. Some have honestly come to the conclusion that they just do not know. Some have been embittered, perhaps by the atrocities committed by fanatically religious people, perhaps by overbearing or abusive parents or religious leaders, or perhaps by a personal tragedy that they cannot reconcile with a God of love. I write to all, for it does not matter how you came to nonbelief. It only matters if you remain there or how and why you may choose to leave.

We have much in common. Our human DNA is 99.9 percent identical, which suggests to me that, like it or not, we are brothers and sisters of one family. We came into being in a particular moment some fourteen billion years after the universe began, and we live together on a small sphere near the edge of a galaxy that is one of many still expanding from each other. While we may disagree as to how or why this came about, we are but tiny dots in space and time. Despite all our human accomplishments—and they are considerable—the death rate for our species remains a constant at 100 percent.

If there is no God, we must find happiness on our own. We must create for ourselves any happiness that may be possible. Likewise, any meaning or purpose, if they should exist at all, must be established by our own endeavors. If there is no God, would this not be a logical conclusion?

Is it not also the case that there is much unhappiness in this passing condition? Much that takes place causes great suffering, and much has no identifiable purpose or greater meaning. Indeed, there is enough misery in life without our adding to it. It would be the height of cruelty or at least highly illogical to engage in behavior that increases our own misery or the misery of others, either by the works of our hands, the words of our mouths, or the attitudes of our hearts. Does this not make sense?

And is it not reasonable to hold that happiness will not be found by turning inward? Turning into ourselves will lead only to isolation and will result in greater misunderstanding and separation. Why would any rational being willingly relinquish any possibility of happiness by turning inward?

Happiness is found by turning outward. It will be found by openness to truth and new understandings. It will be found by helping one another and supporting one another, by letting go of old resentments and seeking peace and harmony. It will be found by genuine caring, self-giving, and acts of kindness.

In a word, any happiness, any meaning or purpose to life, will be found in love. Our opinions and beliefs may be far apart, but our love may be the same.

Do you not see the irony?

When people of faith fail to love, then no matter what they may say or profess, they are not one with that which is love. And when nonbelievers give themselves in love, they are living in the reality of that which is love.

To live in the reality of that which is love is to live in God.

So what is to be gained by persisting in nonbelief?

# Where Was God?

Where was God when my spouse died, when my mother or father died, when my child died? Where was God when the tornado struck my home, when the hurricane leveled my neighborhood, when my doctor told me he could do no more? Where was God when I needed him? Where was God when any tragedy destroys hopes and dreams and life?

The enigma of human suffering is a serious challenge to people of faith. Why suffering? Why pain and misfortune and calamities? Why did it happen to me? If a chain smoker dies of lung cancer, we can rationally understand that our human behavior does have consequences, and that our behavior can be self-destructive. But how do we explain an incurable disease in a child? For centuries, men and women of faith have wrestled with the question, where was God? I have no pretension that I have the knowledge to answer that question. But I do affirm that sacred Scripture has profound insights into human suffering, insights that enable us, in the words of Milton, to "assert eternal providence, and justify the ways of God to men" (*Paradise Lost*, Book I).

**Biblical Insight No. 1: It's Okay to Be Angry**

Anger is a normal response to any loss and frequently accompanies the grief process. To lose your car keys is to experience the minor anger of frustration and inconvenience. To lose a loved one is to experience the deeper anger that comes from a severe pain that will impact the rest of your life. It is okay to be angry, even angry at God. The psalmist cried out, "How long, O LORD? Will you forget me forever? How long will you hide your face from me?" (Psalm 13:1). "How long?" is not a chronological question. The psalmist is not asking, will it be three months, or six months, or a year? It is a cry of the human heart, a cry of deep emotion, a cry of desolation and abandonment. It is an angry cry. It is the psalmist shaking his fist at God and demanding deliverance. It is a human response from the gut. And it is okay. God can take it. Expect that you will experience anger when you suffer loss. It is normal to be angry.

**Biblical Insight No. 2: Bad Things Happen**

We live in a world where good things happen and bad things happen. As Rabbi Kushner reminds us, bad things happen not only to bad people but to good people as well (Harold Kushner, *When Bad Things Happen to Good People*). In the first century AD, a tragedy struck in a town called Siloam. A tower collapsed, and eighteen people were suddenly killed. Jesus asked, "Do you think they were worse offenders than others living in Jerusalem?" (Luke 13:4). Was God punishing these poor victims because they were evil and sparing others because they were good? The answer is no; it just happened. Goodness and disaster come both to the good and to the bad. It is the way of the world. "The Father in heaven makes his sun rise on the evil and on the good, and sends rain to fall on the righteous and on the unrighteous" (Matthew 5:45). In an episode of the television program *Touched by an Angel*, Bill Cosby, who himself experienced a tragic loss, remarked, "Bad things happen; that's all. I wouldn't blame God for the things I don't have. I'd thank God for the things I have."

**Biblical Insight No. 3: God Suffers with Us**

When God summoned Moses to deliver the Hebrew people from slavery, God spoke surprising words: "I have observed the misery of my people who are in Egypt; I have heard their cry on account of their taskmasters. Indeed, I know their sufferings" (Exodus 3:7). God is not aloof from human suffering. God sees, God hears, and God knows. When Cain murdered Abel, God asked Cain, "What have you done?

Listen; your brother's blood is crying to me from the ground!" (Genesis 4:10). Christian faith is centered in Jesus Christ, Emmanuel, God with us, the incarnate God who experiences grief and pain and even death itself from within a human life. Where was God? One answer to that question is this: God was there beside you, experiencing your loss, and crying with you. And that may be helpful to the folks who are angry at God. It is understandable to be angry at a God who sits on a throne in the far corner of the universe and ignores the suffering of humankind. But how can you be angry at a God who hangs on a cross? Who is the god you are angry at? Is it God, or your mistaken projection of what God should be about?

**Biblical Insight No. 4: Suffering Does Not Separate Us from God's Love**

Many things destroy earthly existence, but nothing can destroy God's ultimate purpose for our lives. The eighth chapter of Paul's letter to the Romans should be embedded in the heart and soul of every believer and proclaimed without apology to everyone who suffers. It's affirmation of God's steadfast love and sovereign purpose is unflinching, no matter what disaster may befall us.

"I consider that the sufferings of this present time are not worth comparing with the glory about to be revealed to us" (Romans 8:18). "We know that all things work together for good for those who love God, who are called according to his purpose" Romans 8:28). "For I am convinced that neither death, nor life, nor angels, nor rulers, nor things present, nor things to come, nor powers, nor height, nor depth, nor anything else in all creation, will be able to separate us from the love of God in Christ Jesus our Lord" (Romans 8:38–39).

Paul does not say that "all things are good." Many things are not good. Paul says, "All things work together for good." God's love is steadfast. It will not be defeated or destroyed. Does your human love for your parents, your spouse, or your children come to an end because they die and you see them no more? No, of course not. Your love endures. And so it is with God's love. In that eternal love, we are "more than conquerors" (Romans 8:37).

**Biblical Insight No. 5: Suffering Does Not Have the Final Word**

When you are in a boat during a violent storm, all that you can see is the beating rain, the flapping of the sails, and the surging of the waves. If you could see a bigger picture, you would see that beyond the storm, there are following seas and sunny skies. Faith asks us to see the bigger picture. "See, the home of God is among mortals. He will dwell with them; they will be his peoples, and God himself will be with them; he will wipe away every tear from their eyes. Death will be no more; mourning and crying and pain will be no more, for the first things have passed away" (Revelation 21:3–4).

Suffering is real. It is universal. It cannot be glossed over. But suffering does not have the final word. God has the final word.

There is a brighter day ahead.

# ✪ Power

Power.

Achieved by conflicts in life, it is lost by the conflict with death.

Its rewards are wealth, fame, and security. Who can resist them? These temptations last a lifetime, and they have been ardently pursued in all of recorded history. Religious people are not immune. But these rewards are like the leaves of summer. Not one of them will last.

What power does God have?

Human suffering is a proof for atheists that God cannot be both all-good and all-powerful. If God is good, God has no power. If God has power, God is not good. The point is specious, for power and control are not the same. The parents who give their teenage son or daughter keys to the family car loses all control at that moment. Power is temporarily relinquished but not permanently lost, for parents can retract the privilege at any time. The gift of freedom does not guarantee a fortuitous outcome.

There is a story in Scripture of one who claims to have and promises to give "all the kingdoms of the world, along with their glory and authority"

(Luke 4:3–7). Such a one would have great power and wield immense control. But the one who makes that claim and promise is not God.

The God who calls the universe into being, the God who is the beginning and end of all things, the God who will reign for all eternity is at the same time a God who gives blessings to the poor (Luke 6:20), who dines with tax collectors and sinners (Luke 15:1–2), who bends down to wash the dust from the feet of weary disciples (John 13:5), who struggles up a hill with a cross on his back (John 19:16–17), and who offers the water of the fountain of life to all who are thirsty (John 4:13–14).

And therein is lodged a power that the world can neither give nor take away.

##  Plaster

In the city of Istanbul stands one of the world's great museums, Hagia Sophia. Erected in AD 537 by the Byzantine emperor Justinian, Hagia Sophia was the world's largest cathedral and a center of Christian worship for more than nine hundred years. Its magnificent dome is a high point, both literally and figuratively, of Byzantine architecture, faith, and culture in what was then called Constantinople, a city as great as Rome or Athens. Throughout the cathedral, priceless mosaics of Christ inspired worshippers and gave glory to the second person of the Trinity, the Word (*Logos*), also known as wisdom (*Sophia*). One mosaic, Christ *Pantocrator* (Ruler of All) is an awesome work of art. Christ, seated on a jeweled throne, looks down in blessing, and holds a book on which is inscribed, "Peace be with you; I am the light of the world" (John 20:21; 8:12).

But tragically, the sons and daughters of Abraham have waged war against each other for centuries. So it was in 1453, when the Muslim armies of Mehmed II destroyed Constantinople and sacked the cathedral. Terrified citizens who had sought refuge in the great sanctuary were among the spoil; the old and sick were slaughtered, women and girls were raped, any with health and strength were captured as slaves. Irreplaceable icons, paintings, and artwork were destroyed, and the great mosaics were plastered over. Thick, heavy plaster covered over the face of Christ. It was the end of a civilization and, seemingly, the end of a faith.

But the worship of the one God continued, though in a different way. The cathedral was converted into a mosque, and Islamic relics and calligraphy adorned the walls. For five hundred years, the daily calls to prayer went out, and believers fell to their knees in submission to the one Lord.

With the creation of the modern secular state of Turkey, Ataturk converted the building into a museum in 1935 but reserved a room where both Christian and Muslim believers may pray and meditate. Vast repairs and renovations needed to be made, for time takes its relentless toll on all things made by human hands. The plaster covering the great mosaics had deteriorated and cracked and was falling away. In 1996, the site was listed on the World Monument Fund, and with assistance from American Express, vast renovations were made. The plaster was removed, revealing artistic achievements that had been covered for half a millennium. The beautiful mosaics were carefully restored by gifted artists and craftsmen. Today, the face of Christ shows through, and visitors from all over the world look up in awe.

Christ has had many enemies in this world. When he was only an infant, Herod tried to slay him. Caiaphas and Pilate tried to slay him. Lenin and Stalin and Hitler tried to slay him. Today, anti-theists try to slay him. They try to cover him over with thick plaster, to remove him from sight and mind, to purge the world of his influence. Some try, with painstaking efforts, to apply layers of plaster, one on top of another, covering every possible place where a bit of awe-inspiring beauty might show through. For them, their arguments are logical and right, designed to remove the world of an ignorant superstition. Others simply hurl handfuls of plaster, in rage or anger, motivated more by bitterness than by any serious search for truth. All cake on the plaster with an arrogant self-righteousness that even the most zealous religious fanatic could not equal.

But let there be no mistake. Truth can be covered but only for a moment. The light shines in the darkness and the darkness can never overcome it (John 1:5).

Plaster cracks and breaks away and lies in dusty rubble on the floor. The face of Christ shows through.

## ❂ The Moron

In the front of most churches, occupying the very center of focus, amid the beautiful stained glass, the freshly cut flowers, and the rich color of the carpet, is a shocking and hideous symbol: a cross. The cross may have Christ hanging on it, or it may be bare, but in both cases, it is a gruesome image of death. It is no different from having a hangman's noose, an electric chair, or a guillotine in the front of a sanctuary devoted to prayer and to praise. You might think that Christians could find something better to adorn their houses of worship. Perhaps a big smiley face. Or a blown-up one-hundred–dollar bill. Or a stock certificate. Or the photo of the Super Bowl MVP, or the most curvaceous movie starlet.

What foolishness, to have a cross at the center of attention! What offensive nonsense! That is what Saint Paul called Christ crucified: "stumbling block to Jews and foolishness to Gentiles" (1 Corinthians 1:23). The word that Paul used in the Greek text for "stumbling block" is *skandalon*, a scandal. The Savior of the world, crucified between two thieves? Scandalous! The Lord of Lords, executed like a criminal? Foolishness! It was true in Paul's day, and it is true in ours as well.

But the cross is not a decoration. It is the intentional reminder of an excruciating death, a word that is derived from the Latin word for cross, *crucis*. Jesus did not die in the soft bed of a nursing home at age 101. He died in the prime of his life, ridiculed, beaten, and spit upon.

What does it mean to look to the cross?

It does not mean that if you do all the right things and behave in all the right ways, you will be saved. It does not mean that if you believe all the right doctrines and worship in the proper manner, then God will love you. It is to rely upon a piece of incredibly good news: the almighty God loves us and cares for us so much that in Jesus Christ, he died on a cross for us. He loves us that much.

Christ did not die because of a few little imperfections in our nature. He did not die because of an occasional flaw or a minor dysfunction in our character. He died because we were lost in sin and death. Sin is not something "out there" in the bad guys. Sin is deep inside, lurking in the depths of every soul. Christ died to set us free from the power of sin that reigns over us and, in setting us free, to transform us to a new being, to his own glorious likeness.

Foolishness? Yes, for those who are perishing. But it is the power of God for those who are being saved (1 Corinthians 1:18).

The Greek word that Paul used for "foolishness" is *moria*. Our English word "moron" is derived from it. It is as if Paul is saying that from the standpoint of the world, you would have to be a moron to preach Christ crucified. And you would have to be a bigger moron to believe it.

If that is the case, I proudly and unashamedly confess that I am the moron. And I invite you to be a moron too.

It may seem like foolishness. But it is the only thing that can save us.

# Time

All earthly beings are creatures in time. Our lives are regulated by time, defined by time, and limited in time. Time has dominion over us.

We are regulated by time. Time is the master of our daily activities. The alarm clock rings, and we arise at an appointed time. We report for school or work or a meeting or a social gathering at an appointed time. We eat our meals at an appointed time. We go to bed at an appointed time. If we should enjoy the privilege of air travel to distant time zones, we temporarily find ourselves disoriented and out of step with the progression of life around us.

We are defined by time. We are living in a specific period in human history. We did not choose the century of our birth. Without our consent, we came into being in a certain moment in time. Our lives would be vastly different had we lived when the great ice ages were covering the hemispheres with glaciers, or when Bronze Age humans were first beginning to fashion tools and weapons from metal, or when Latin and Greek were the primary languages of the Western world, or when fifteenth-century Italian painters were initiating a renaissance of cultured civilization, or even when the first machines of the Industrial Revolution were changing the way we reap our grain. Our lives are shaped by living in our "now."

We are limited in time. From infants wholly dependent on the nurture and care of others to the last dying moments before we return to the dust of the earth, our lives are brief and passing. "We flourish like a flower of the field; the wind passes over it and it is gone, and its place knows it no more" (Psalm 103:15-16). And it is not only our personal lives that are limited in time: all our human institutions, all our human empires, and all our human accomplishments and achievements either have slipped or one day will slip into the abyss of nothingness.

All people, without exception, are subjects of time. Time is the master over all of us. Yet all people, without exception may embrace the Eternal. Jews have understood this by loving, with all the heart, mind, and strength, the sovereign Lord who delivered their mothers and fathers out of bondage. Christians have discovered this in an incarnate Word that became flesh and dwelt among us, demonstrating that love will never end. Muslims have realized this by faith, prayer, alms, fasting, and pilgrimage. Hindus and Buddhists and countless others have experienced this by relinquishing self and meditating upon the supreme reality that is beyond everything in this world.

There is no earthly way to find liberation from the dominion of time. Only by embracing the Eternal, only in relationship with that which is beyond time, will our lives have meaning and purpose. Call it Yahweh, call it Allah, call it Brahman, call it Father, or call it what you will. Apart from the One who is transcendent over time, we quickly pass through our brief lives and, like the leaf falling from the tree, fade into oblivion.

# ❂ The Leaf

As a devoted believer, I wish I could formulate a proof for the existence of God. I dearly wish that one of these offerings would be a rationale so persuasive that the agnostic would come to knowledge, the indifferent would be moved to worship, and even the most rigid atheist would come to faith.

Perhaps God does not desire a proof of his existence. God may well want his sons and daughters to trust him like a little child and not insist on a demonstrable certainty contrived by human reason.

Nonetheless, there is something within me that would like to reach out to dear brothers and sisters who do not believe with convincing proof. But I do not have the genius of an Anselm or an Aquinas, so my wish has not come to pass.

However, there is one whose witness to the reality of God is so intricate, so complex yet so simple, so beautiful, and so profound that it must be taken seriously.

On a beautiful October day in Catoctin State Park in West Virginia, I picked up a golden leaf. Not long before that day, it had been a bud in the gentle rains of April. Then it burst forth as a leaf, not golden, but with a light and delicate green hue. As cool mornings gave way to the heat of summer, the light green color changed to a dark, deep, and vibrant green. Then, with the coming of early morning frost, the leaf took on the eye-catching gold that I held in my hand.

It was a thing of astonishing beauty. As I looked upon it, I saw the tiny veins that carried the nourishment that gave it life. Turning the leaf over, I saw even smaller veins, and as I looked more closely, I saw even smaller veins and then a vast network of even tinier capillaries, barely visible to the human eye. I was amazed at the evolutionary process that, over billions of years, resulted in such advanced structure. But surely it is more than an evolutionary process. Can there be any doubt that mind-boggling engineering lay behind this golden marvel of creation?

It was but one leaf from a tree with countless leaves, on a mountain with countless trees, in a state where the mountains seem to stretch forever. I held it in my hand for a brief moment and then let it fall to the earth from which it came, where it would provide nourishment for leaves that would adorn the forest for generations yet to come. It spoke no words, but its witness speaks more clearly than all the utterances I have ever made.

For if the entire universe consisted of nothing but that one golden leaf, I would be compelled to believe in a marvelous Creator.

## ❁ Take a Walk

For thousands of years, pilgrimages have been sacred for the world's great religions.

Bodh Gaya, the place where Siddhartha Gautama received enlightenment, is sacred to followers of Buddha. The waters of the Ganges purify Hindus during Kumbh Mela; over 100 million people participated in 2013. Muslims center on Mecca during the Hajj, one of the five pillars of the faith of Islam. Christians have gone to the Church of the Holy Sepulchre or, with Chaucer's famous pilgrims, have venerated the tomb of Thomas Becket in Canterbury. Jews come to the Wailing Wall, the retaining wall from the Jerusalem Temple destroyed by Rome in AD 70, to pray both aloud and silently by placing small pieces of paper with written prayers in the cracks between the great stones.

I think these pilgrims of every time and every religion are on to something. Traditionally they have walked, sometimes for hundreds of miles. Perhaps the walk is as sacred as the actual moment of veneration at a revered shrine.

There is something sacred about walking, something that brings healing to body and soul, something that conveys peace and freshness, something sacramental. Not the rushed and frantic walk in and out of a busy grocery store or the hurried walk to get to an appointment on time. But the slow, casual stroll, when you take time to see the blue sky and golden daffodils, warmly say hello to a passing stranger, notice the strata of rocks that are billions of years old, hear the soft crunch of autumn leaves under your feet, or pause by a flowering cherry tree to tell it that it's doing a good job.

The word for that slow, casual walk is the English word saunter. It derives from the French, *sainte terre*, which literally means holy land, holy ground. To saunter is holy. It is a time to experience the Holy One in our midst. Indeed, if only we realized it, all of life is holy. To be born, to breathe, to be baptized, to run and play leapfrog, to study, to marry, to break bread, to play a game of catch with a grandchild, to grow old, to die—it is holy. It is all holy.

That which is beyond this world is present in this world, at all times and in all places. It takes faith and sensitivity to understand that; it may take a walk to experience it.

We are standing on holy ground (Exodus 3:5).

Take a walk.

# Remember

Of all the diseases that afflict humankind, surely Alzheimer's is among the very worst. How terribly sad it would be not to be able to remember. And it is more than forgetting where you left your car keys. That is fairly normal, not Alzheimer's. But when you are holding your keys in your hand and do not know what they are, that is severe disease. It is the total breakdown of memory and experience. It is the loss of all past associations, so the world around you makes no sense. You don't know where you came from, who your parents were, what you did for a living, or how to find your way home. Your husband or wife may look familiar to you, but you don't know who that person is. You may not even know your own name. What a frightening and lonely experience to be completely cut off from your past, cut off from your relationships, and cut off from everything that makes life coherent, orderly, and enjoyable. What a disabling and disorienting condition that would be!

Is there not a condition of modern life that might be accurately described as spiritual Alzheimer's? And would it not be as disabling as the physical condition? Not to understand that it is God who has made us and not we ourselves (Psalm 100:3); not to know where we have come from as a people of God; not to realize that the story of the Bible is our story; not to know in our hearts that we are part of a people that has been saved and redeemed by the mighty act of God in Jesus Christ; not to comprehend—that would be truly disabling. It is to lose our identity. It is to lose our purpose in life. Like an Alzheimer's patient, we can no longer make sense out of reality. We see ourselves as insignificant by-products of an accidental universe.

One of the oldest commandments of the Hebrew people is to "observe the Sabbath day and keep it holy" (Deuteronomy 5:12). The rationale for this commandment, in Deuteronomy, is to remember who you are and where you have come from: "Remember that you were a slave in the land of Egypt, and the Lord your God brought you out from there with a mighty hand and an outstretched arm; therefore the Lord your God commanded you to keep the Sabbath day" (Deuteronomy 5:15).

Every Jew in every generation must see himself or herself as having been delivered by the mighty act of God. What happened at the Red Sea has happened for every Jew in every age. Remember, O son or daughter of Israel, who you are! You were nothing! You were like dust under Pharaoh's chariot wheels. Troubled and afflicted, you slaved away in Pharaoh's brickyard. No one cared. No one was concerned. But the God of Abraham cared. God came down to deliver you. Let the Sabbath day be a special day, a day to remember and give thanks. Not to give thanks for what God has done is to be a miserable and ungrateful wretch.

In the same way, every Christian of every generation must see himself or herself as having been delivered from sin and death by the crucifixion and resurrection of Jesus Christ. What happened on that hill in Jerusalem has happened to us and for us. It is our story. It defines us. It is who we are. Every Sunday, the day of resurrection, is a day of celebration. Every Sunday, when the first rays of light dawn on the far horizon, we remember the sunrise on that day of resurrection, when a few frightened women went to the tomb of Jesus and found it empty. We remember that good news: "He is not here! He has been raised!" (Mark 16:6). We remember that Christ is alive and that he lives forevermore (Revelation 1:17–18).

On the first day of the week we hear the Scriptures read, we sing the hymns, we enjoy the music, we offer our gifts, and we greet our friends. But most of all, we remember. We remember the acts of God, the will of God, the promises of God, the grace of God, the call of God, and the victory of God. We remember that we belong to God. We are his. We remember and give thanks.

## Be Strong

> "Be strong in the Lord, and in the strength of his power" (Ephesians 6:10).

These are words that everyone needs to hear.

Parents need to hear these words. It is an awesome responsibility to be a parent. Somehow, you have to survive sleepless nights, dirty diapers, the terrible twos, the growing-up years, going on dates, loud music, body piercing, hair dyed with purple Kool-Aid, and learning how to drive. You have to pay an immense sum of money to feed, clothe, and educate each child; heal a broken bone or two; and suffer through innumerable colds, flu, and chicken pox. And then comes the hardest part of all. After eighteen or twenty years of giving up everything you have for your children, you have to let them go with a smile and a stiff upper lip. It is an awesome responsibility to be a parent. Every parent needs to hear the words, be strong.

Married couples need to hear these words. Being married is more than a romantic meal with candlelight and a glass of wine. It is a covenant of love and faithfulness that hangs in there even when there are tensions and pressures, arguments and power plays, control issues and conflicts of interest. Marriage means giving and caring and sharing and listening and being there for one another. Marriage takes work—the hard effort required to be a reconciler and peace maker. And every marriage will end in pain. Whether it ends by divorce or by death, you cannot put asunder what God has joined together without pain. Every married couple needs to hear the words, be strong.

Children need to hear these words. Even young children live with anxieties, the fear of being abandoned, or the terror of the monster lurking in the closet when the lights are turned out. Students live in world filled with temptations, from cheating on a test, to trying a smoke, to having a drink or fooling around with drugs, to experimenting with a sexual fling. Every student needs to realize it is the weak person who goes along with the crowd and gives in to temptation. It is the strong person who stands firm on his/her principles and convictions. Every student needs to hear the words, be strong.

Older adults need to hear these words. Declining health and failing vision or hearing bring about a new set of anxieties. There is the constant concern of whether a limited income will adequately meet the rising cost of living. And there are important questions to be answered. How much longer can I continue to drive a car? Should I remain in my home, or should I move to an assisted living facility? How can I best manage my financial assets? Older adults need to hear the words, be strong.

Actually, the Scripture does not say, "Be strong." It says, "Be strong in the Lord and in the strength of his power." Our strength is a derived strength. It comes from the Lord. On our own, our strength is weak and shaky. Our strength is like the light of the moon. There is something extremely beautiful about moonlight, especially when the moon is full, and the sky is clear. But the moon has no light of its own. Its light comes from beyond itself, from the sun. Any strength we have comes from beyond ourselves. "Our help is in the name of the Lord, who made heaven and earth" (Psalm 124:8).

We do not rely on the empty power of a finite source or on the vain promise of one who is unable to deliver. We place our confidence in the One who created the heavens and the earth and who holds in his hands the destiny of all things, from the tiniest quark to the greatest galaxy.

There will come a time when every nation and empire will be no more, when the mountains and hills will have eroded to dust, when every human culture and institution will have passed away, and when all biological life will have become extinct, yet those who are in Christ will be alive. They will outlive the universe. They have been given the certainty of eternal life. They have been given the power to become children of God (John 1:6). "Heaven and earth will pass away, but my words will not pass away" (Mark 13:31). The Word of God will stand forever.

Be strong!

# The Apple Tree

There is an apple tree that grows in the garden. I don't know how old the apple tree might be, but it is very old. It is a marvelous tree. I love its lovely blossoms in the springtime and its laden branches in the fall. I love to sit in its shade on a hot summer day and admire its magnificence. I love the apple tree, and I love to tell others about it.

One day, I told my friend about the apple tree. He did not seem to be quite as ecstatic about the tree as I am. "I have seen rotten apples," he told me. "In fact, I have seen a lot of rotten apples."

"Yes," I said, admitting to the truth of his statement. "When apples fall to the dust of the ground, they are badly bruised and marred. Flies and wasps swarm around them. They are quickly discolored and become quite rotten."

"So the ground is littered with spoiled apples?" he asked me.

"Yes, I'm afraid that it is."

"Then it seems to me," my friend said, "that there is only one conclusion that can be drawn. There is no good apple tree. A good apple tree does not exist. Or if in the slim probability that there is such a tree, it needs to be cut down. Anyone who believes in such a tree suffers from a delusion."

Our conversation is yet to be resolved. My friend is too far removed to see the apple tree. And I completely fail to understand how there is any logical connection between bad apples, that are surely there, and the existence of the magnificent tree that towers over the garden.

##  Women

In the Semitic world of the first century AD, the lives of women were—to be generous—subject to men. Women remained silent in the synagogue and were separated from worshipping men. Women did not learn to read and write or to learn the Scripture; a rabbi's students were all boys. When a young woman was old enough to be married, often while still in her teens, the marriage was brokered and bartered by her father. The bride had no say in whom or how old her husband might be. Women did not work outside the home; they baked the bread, carried the water from the village well, prepared the flax for clothing, tended the domestic animals, and provided for the needs of the husband and the children. Women were forbidden from being witnesses in a court of law, presumably on the grounds that women would not get the story straight, or would be distracted by gossip and hearsay, or would be too emotionally unstable to offer a reliable testimony.

In this context, the good news of Jesus' resurrection is a shocking surprise and not only because the tomb could not contain him. All four Gospels are quite clear that the people who first proclaimed that Jesus had been raised from the dead were women.

The resurrection is central to the Christian faith. It is a defining event for Christians, the beginning of a new creation and the defeat of the powers of sin and death by the God who became flesh and dwelt among us. When Paul wrote to the early church in Corinth, he went so far as to argue that if Christ has not been raised, faith is futile. We are still under the dominion of sin, and those who have died are indeed dead. If Christ has not been raised, then his followers are, of all people, the most to be pitied (1 Corinthians 15:17–19). What may be the earliest creed in Christianity simply states, "Christ died for our sins in accordance with the

Scriptures, and that he was buried, and that he was raised on the third day in accordance with the Scriptures" (1 Corinthians 15:3–4).

Now, if the resurrection is central to Christianity, one might assume that the leaders of the early church would ensure that this good news would be conveyed in a way that would lead to no uncertainty, no doubt, no possible confusion, and no possibility of denial or dispute. If the story were a fabrication, perhaps to keep their movement alive, the early followers of Jesus would have gone to great lengths to reduce the chance that anyone could call their story into question. In other words, if the story were a fabrication, there is no way that women would have been the first preachers of a new faith.

When a woman said, "I have seen the Lord" (John 20:18), and when women told the disciples, "Don't be afraid; go to Galilee and there you will see him" (Matthew 28:10), it was a striking confirmation that Jesus really was raised from the dead. From the viewpoint of male disciples, "it was an idle tale, and they did not believe them" (Luke 24:11). Indeed one man would not believe until he could see and touch the wounds of crucifixion, causing the Lord to make a promise, "Blessed are those who have not seen, and yet who have come to believe" (John 20:29).

Women saw, believed, and proclaimed good news. Why would we deny them that witness?

## ✺ The Bird Feeder

It brings me both joy and sadness. Filled with millet and sunflower seeds, a bird feeder hangs in my back yard. Cardinals, sparrows, nuthatches, finches, and jays all come to feed, and I rejoice to see them—except when the day is ending, and the light is beginning to fade. The birds all come at that time, perhaps for their equivalent of a late-evening supper or a midnight snack. And the phrase "pecking order" is manifested without mercy. Sadly, I watch the bigger birds land at the feeder and drive off the smaller birds. If a finch or sparrow endeavors to land and feed beside a jay or cardinal, it is quickly sent on its way. Even female cardinals are driven away by the males. When the males and bigger birds have had their fill, the smaller and female birds may come and dine.

Do they not know that day by day there is seed within the feeder? Do they not understand that when the feeder empties, I shall come and fill it? It brings me joy to see the birds; I shall not let the feeder go unfilled. It is my desire that not one of them goes hungry.

And is not God disturbed when, in our greed, we deprive the weaker neighbors of our human flock the grains and fruits that spring forth so abundantly from out of this good earth?

## Holy War

It is time to wage holy war.

On September 11, 2001, religious fanatics waged what has been termed *jihad* against the United States of America, murdering nearly three thousand innocent people. In addition to those killed in the four airplanes, at the Pentagon, and in the crashing towers, 411 fire fighters police, and other emergency workers died, trying to save the victims. *Jihad* was waged not only against the United States but against the world. For the World Trade Center was truly a *world* trade center. Victims from twenty-three countries were included in the list of the dead. If someone wants to know what *jihad* is, we must show them what *jihad* is. It is time for holy war.

Let there be no mistake. This must not be a half-hearted effort. This must be all-out war. There can be no holding back and no surrender. There must be a total commitment behind this endeavor, and the time to wage war is now.

No, this is not a call to arms. It is a call for holy war, and if a war is truly "holy," it cannot involve violence. There is no place for killing in a holy war. A holy war can tolerate no enmity, no retaliation, and no settling of the score. A war that is holy does not utilize guns and bombs—bullets, and IEDs by the side of the road. This must be a war against evil, and evil is not defeated by evil's methodologies, nor by reducing ourselves to the level of madmen.

When will the peoples of the world learn an age-old truth? "Our struggle is not against enemies of blood and flesh" (Ephesians 6:12a). Our struggle is not against other people. Although people bring great harm against us, the ultimate struggle is not with them. Our struggle is against the powers of darkness, the forces of evil, and the destructive sins of pride and greed, of hatred and revenge. A war that is holy must be waged with love and righteousness, with truth and justice, and with words of forgiveness and deeds of love and kindness.

The word *jihad* literally means "struggle"—a struggle in the ways of Allah. And surely Allah desires that his people live together in peace, practicing the mercy that is one of Allah's qualities. Cannot reasonable people of every faith work together in a common struggle—against hunger and poverty, against oppression and persecution, against sickness and disease of both mind and body?

For thousands of years, humans have waged war. It is time to admit that the ways of the past are not working. It is time to end the bloodshed and to unite in a new struggle.

It is time to wage holy war.

## The Work of Religion

Religion takes work.

I say that as a committed, old-fashioned, dyed-in-the-wool Protestant. I stand with Luther in being absolutely convinced that we are justified by grace through faith (Ephesians 2:8). What that means is that our relationship with God is not based on what we do or how good we happen to be. We are loved by God and accepted by God simply because God loves and not by any merit of our own. We do not have to earn God's approval or win our way into God's favor. It is a matter of grace, not work. It is all by grace.

Nonetheless, I believe that religion is work. Everything about religion is work. Religion is not sentimentality or a warm, fuzzy feeling that somewhere there is a God. It is not a casual indifference to the command that we be "doers of the word, and not merely hearers who deceive themselves" (James 1:22). Religion is work—hard work; dedicated work and effort. And if we are not working at our religion, our religion is weak and wimpy.

Reading Scripture is work. I do not believe that you can casually pick up a Bible, randomly turn to a page, and expect to get very much out of it. I know that I cannot. I need to study, to sit in a classroom and listen to a teacher, to read the commentaries, and to consult the dictionaries and study helps. More than that, I need to open my life to the Word of God and allow it to transform my life. I need to be receptive to what God may be saying to me through the printed text. And that takes work.

Praying takes work. Prayer requires intensity, concentration, and energy. I sometimes catch myself babbling as I pray, just reciting words and phrases without giving it much thought. I have to tell myself, *Stop babbling and pray!* Perhaps you have found yourself babbling as well. When I pray I must understand that I am in the presence of an awesome God. I must realize that I am living under the dominion of sin and death and that I desperately need a merciful Savior. When I pray for others, I must see them as my brothers and sisters who are finite, dying, and in need of grace, just like me. I can no longer look down upon them, or despise them, or hold a grudge in my heart against them. I must see their need, have compassion upon them, and commend them to the Father's care. I must allow my heart to go out to them. And that takes work.

Love takes work. How do I love in a world of overwhelming need, a world where millions are malnourished or sick or refugees? How do I love the tragic victims of hurricanes and tornados, earthquakes, and floods? How do I love the children caught in the crossfire of warfare, whose life may be cut short at any moment by bullets and bombs? How do I love the beggar in my own hometown? Is it not by sharing, by giving, by seeking justice, by lending a helping hand, and by reaching out with my resources? Actually, they are not my resources; they are God's. My money, my talents, my abilities, my skills, and my time all are gifts of God, and all are given in abundance that I might engage in the work of love. It takes work to love the needy of the world.

Actually, it takes work to love my neighbors, my friends, and even my family. Peace and harmony do not come automatically. It takes listening and communicating and not just in following my own agenda. It takes compromise and seeking the win/win and not insisting on my own way. It takes patience and commitment and hanging in there when the going gets rough. It takes love to hold relationships together; without love, relationships will deteriorate and fall apart. And that takes work.

What is religion? Jesus' brother, James, defined religion for us: "Religion that is pure and undefiled before God the Father, is this: to care for the orphans and widows in their distress, and to keep oneself unstained by the world" (James 1:27).

In this world, there is much work to be done. It is the work of religion.

May God's people everywhere stop fighting among themselves. May they end their senseless bickering and self-righteousness. May they relinquish the mentality that we are right and those who do not think as we do are wrong. May they put down their weapons and pick up their hammers and saws, their bandages and medicines, their tablets and cell phones, their mixing bowls and measuring cups—whatever their tools of labor may be.

The holiday is over. It is time to go to work.

# ✿ Risky Giving

I don't like to take a risk. I am not a risky kind of guy. When I go on vacation, I want to know in advance where I will spend each night. I carefully go online, study the lodging options and costs, and make my reservations well in advance. And of course, I want to make sure that the room is nonsmoking and that breakfast is included. When I make a big purchase, I very closely examine my checkbook and make certain I can handle the payments that must be made each month. No risks for me. When I go to an amusement park, I head straight for the merry-go-round. There is no way I am going to get on the ride that flips me over, spins me around, and accelerates me in the downward direction at seventy miles an hour. I am reserved, calculating, methodical, practical, and safe.

In all of this, I am like the disciples of Jesus. Had I been there, I would have shared their anger and joined in their protest.

It was just day or two before the Last Supper, perhaps a next-to-the-Last Supper (Matthew 26:6–16). Jesus and his disciples had gone to home of a leper for dinner. It was a radically risky thing to do. Simon was not a recovering leper or a healed leper; he was a leper. Where once there were fingers, now there were stubs. Where once there was a clear complexion, now there was rotting flesh. For good reason, the ancient Hebrew law contained a prohibition against socializing with lepers (Leviticus 13:45–46). Yet Jesus took the risk. While they were at dinner, a woman entered the house, apparently uninvited, and took a risk so outrageous that it was bound to provoke criticism. She broke open an alabaster jar of perfume and poured it over the head and body of Jesus—not a little dab behind the ears or a tiny drop rubbed into the wrists, the way you might normally apply perfume. She broke the jar open and poured it all out. The perfume was extremely expensive, worth three hundred *denarii*, an amount that equaled nearly a year's pay for the average worker (Mark 14:5). The disciples were angered, for the perfume could have been sold and the money used to help the poor. That makes sense to me. Why be so wasteful? For Judas, it was the straw that broke the camel's back, and he went to the chief priests to betray Jesus (Matthew 26:14). But Jesus praised the woman: "She has performed a good service for me" (Matthew 26:10).

Love is not calculating. Love does not count the cost. Love breaks the boundaries of common sense. Love gives and pours and flows in abundance. It is lavish, extravagant, and yes, even reckless. It does not hold back; it is not restrained. Love is not a miserly disciple, like me. Love is a woman who pours out her perfume and a man on a cross whose blood is poured out and given freely.

A man and his son approached the cashier in a large grocery store to pay for the numerous items spread out on the belt. "Would you like to contribute one dollar to help the hungry?" the cashier asked him. The man knew that you cannot respond to every request for help, so he politely declined. The son, behind him in line, said, "I will give a dollar." The father turned to him "Do you have some money?" he asked.

"Yes."

"How much money do you have?"

"A dollar."

Bear in mind that every imaginable candy bar that any boy would ever want was invitingly displayed by the grocery store cashier. But this boy was prepared to give his dollar. I did not make up this story; I know it to be true. The man was my son; the boy, my grandson. My son was trained by me. He knew he must be careful, responsible, cautious, and restrained. My grandson was an example of sheer love, eager to help. Perhaps this is why Jesus said, "Whoever does not receive the kingdom of God as a little child will never enter it" (Mark 10:15).

There is an urgency to love. Jesus was about to die. His body was being prepared for burial (Matthew 26:12). Had the woman procrastinated, she would have been too late.

Tomorrow may be the most dangerous word in the English language, for tomorrow may never come. When is the time to give love to others? Now is the time. When is the time to "hate what is evil and hold fast to what is good" (Romans 12:9)? Now is the time. When is the time to bind up the wounded and heal the broken-hearted, to feed the hungry and shelter the homeless, and offer a cup of cold water to the thirsty? Now is the time. When is the time to be citizens of a new creation, ambassadors of reconciliation in a broken world? Now is the time. When is the time to turn to Jesus and to follow in his way? Now is the time. When is the time to write that note, to send those flowers, to offer that apology, or to let someone know you love him or her? Now is the time (2 Corinthians 6:2). Don't wait until you get out of school, until your children grow up, until you get a better job, until you retire—until whatever. Do it now.

Normally, I would encourage you to be like the disciples. I might, in an egotistical lapse of sense, invite you to be like me. But the proper advice is, do not be like the disciples and, most assuredly, do not be like me.

Take a risk! Break open the jar! Let the perfume pour out freely and abundantly! Breathe deeply of the rich aroma! Let your love be lavish!

The woman did a beautiful thing for Jesus. And we can do it too.

## Treasures in Unexpected Places

He went to the church alone, often late at night. It was not to pray, although he was a man of prayer. He went to change the burned-out light bulbs, perform some handyman repairs, or complete any of the constant little odd jobs that must be done to keep any building functioning. He finished his work and left the church, carefully locking the door behind him. Safe by day, this neighborhood bore signs of frequent vandalism at night—boarded-up shops, metallic grates protecting doors and windows, graffiti-covered walls.

In front of the church was a large "skip," the term this old Irishman used for a Dumpster. It was filled with trash from the restaurant next door, which was under renovation. Construction debris and scraps of drywall and lumber filled the skip, along with numerous items being discarded by the restaurant owners. Something caught his eye—a dented pitcher, blackened and badly tarnished from years of non-use. He took it home and began to clean it. As he worked, he realized it was silver. With much effort, lots of metal polish, and even some WD-40, he restored it to a beautiful silver pitcher. And to his great surprise, he saw etching that revealed its age and identity. It was a communion pitcher, used to pour wine into a chalice. It had been given to his church more than a hundred years earlier.

(This is a true story. I was the pastor of this congregation in Bangor, Northern Ireland, at the time the discarded vessel was discovered. I confess that my wife and I also removed some items from the skip: a set of old chairs that could be used in the manse. We asked permission of the restaurant owner before taking them and then removed them in broad daylight. A parishioner saw us diving in the skip and, of course, we skip-divers became the brunt of many jokes.)

Is there not a lesson here for all of us? What we think may be refuse may actually be of value. What we consider trash may be a precious treasure. The Dead Sea Scrolls were discovered in clay jars. And a sacred vessel that held the blood of Christ was found in a common Dumpster.

Paul spoke of a very precious treasure when he referred to "the light of the gospel of the glory of Christ" (2 Corinthians 4:4). There is a light that shines in this dark world, a light that brings hope to the hopeless and life to the dying (John 1:4-5). It is a precious treasure. "But we have this treasure in clay jars," Paul wrote, "so that it may be made clear that this extraordinary power belongs to God, and does not come from us" (2 Corinthians 4:7). Paul was describing his ministry or indeed, the ministry of anyone. A finite, sinful human can share with others a gift of infinite worth—the light of the gospel of the glory of Christ. The clergy who serve your church, synagogue, or mosque are not perfect. They are clay jars. Yet they have a treasure to share, even as the Dead Sea Scrolls were found in the clay jars of wilderness caves.

The Bible is full of examples. An adulterer and murderer, King David, unified God's people and sang God's praise in magnificent psalms (2 Samuel 7:1–17). A cheating and thieving tax collector, Zacchaeus, repented, restored fourfold what he had stolen, and gave half of his possessions to the poor (Luke 19:1–10). A fisherman who denied Christ, Simon Peter, became the first pope (Mark 14:66–72). And the man who spread Christian faith throughout vast regions of Asia Minor and Europe, Paul, was once a terrorist. Yes, that is the proper description, for he literally went from house to house and dragged Christians from their homes to persecute them (Acts 8:1–3).

What does this say to our lives? Could it be that we—common and ordinary people, stained by sins and errors of the past—might yet contain a precious treasure? Never think that there is not a saving light that could shine forth from your life. Never hide the light of the gospel of the glory of Christ. Never hold back your love. Never underestimate what you could do. And what of others? We may consider them to be fallen and full of sin, we may judge them to be trash. And our judgment may be accurate. But there may be a precious treasure within them. Never give up on someone. Never stop seeking and praying for someone's redemption. Never be so hardened that you cannot reach out with love and grace.

Stay alert. Keep your minds and your hearts open.

For treasures may be found in unexpected places.

## Second Diversion

Memories of my childhood are real and often very vivid. A little boy, riding his bicycle to play baseball with his friends; hunting for soda bottles in the town park to retrieve the seemingly enormous deposit of two cents per bottle; summer evenings sitting in the backyard, listening to Phillies games with my dad; teasing my younger sister mercilessly (a practice I now deeply regret); watching my mother wring out wet laundry using a roller wringer on an early washing machine and then hanging damp clothing on an outdoor line; crawling under a desk with my hand cradled over my head when an air-raid drill was announced, a fearful exercise that took place as regularly as the customary fire drills.

I have no doubt that the little boy in those memories is me. It is not my memory of another child, real or make-believe; that little boy is me. And here is the amazing thing. Science tells me that there is not one cell, not one atom, currently in my body or brain that was there when I was a child. How are experiences preserved and remembered? By what process are they kept alive? I assume that science will discover the mystery by which this phenomenon may take place. But is it not yet another sign that human life is more than merely matter and energy, more than hydrocarbons and electrical impulses?

The news of the world was steeped in war on March 14, 1943. The German army had retaken the Ukrainian port of Kharkov after a major offensive. And Nazi persecutors had "liquidated" the Krakow ghetto, killing in the streets or sending off to Auschwitz two thousand Jewish men, women, and children. The Krupp factory in Essen was in flames after one thousand tons of bombs were dropped by RAF bombers. HMS *Thunderbolt* was sunk off the coast of Sicily, killing all on board. And in the Pacific, American Flying Fortresses attacked a Japanese convoy, hitting two large cargo ships. Not all of the news was troubling. The Detroit Red Wings were still playing hockey, and led the Boston Bruins by four points. Aaron Copeland's *Fanfare for the Common Man* premiered in New York. And in Harrisburg, Pennsylvania, a common man was born: Paul Byron Brought. (For the first years of my life, I was called both Skippy and Barry; when I enrolled in school, my parents asked me what I wanted to be called, and I said Byron, and that became my name.) The birth took place on a Sunday morning; someone called the church, and the announcement was made in the worship service.

Throughout my childhood, my parents gave my sister and me great care, nurturing, and love. They consistently and dependably acted in our best interest. Two experiences come to mind that relate my childhood to the times.

In 1955, Jonas Salk developed a vaccine that could prevent polio. Prior to that, polio was a leading health menace in the nation. In 1952, there were fifty-eight thousand cases of the disease, taking the lives of over three thousand and leaving more than twenty-one thousand paralyzed, most of them children. Treatment included prolonged periods in an "iron lung," as the illness took away both health and freedom of mobility. As a child, I was prohibited from swimming in a city swimming pool. My parents believed that swimming in a public pool was a way to contract the disease. While it seemed restrictive at the time, I know they were carefully guarding my life.

My parents made a big financial purchase when I was nearly nine years old: a television set. I have no idea what they paid for it, but I'm sure it was a difficult decision to spend so much money for a TV. The set was black-and-white, of course, with perhaps a ten- or twelve-inch screen and could receive only one channel. Reception was blurry, and we often had the impression we were watching the action through a snowstorm. The reason they purchased the TV is so that my sister and I could watch the accession of Queen Elizabeth II in February 1952 and follow the national presidential election that would unfold that year, Eisenhower vs. Stevenson. It was one of many sacrifices my parents made so that Barbara and I could receive an education.

Our home was a modest, three-bedroom double house in Paxtang, a suburb of Harrisburg. We were privileged to live in a safe community, with pleasant neighbors, and a good school system. In my younger years, we did not have a car; my father rode the bus to work, and I remember watching for him to arrive at the bus stop in the late afternoons and running down the hill to greet him. From a young age, I worked to earn some money, mowing lawns and shoveling snow in the neighborhood and delivering a weekly newspaper, the *Home Star,* to three hundred homes every Wednesday afternoon. My pay was $1.50 per week. Often, my mother had to borrow that money to pay for groceries, but she always paid it back. My bedroom overlooked the backyard, which gave rise to what is probably the first experience of fear that I can remember. We had a pet rabbit that lived in a small hutch in the backyard. I could see it clearly from my window. There was an older boy in town who would tell me daily that the bogeyman would come to get my rabbit. Of course, I believed it. So at night, when I should have been peacefully sleeping, I would watch out my window, scared to death, for the bogeyman to come. How fearful we are over things that never happen!

Faith was central to our family and included the usual practices: grace before meals, weekly worship and education, and a festive observance of Christmas, Thanksgiving, and Easter, both in church and in the home. Dad had a fantastic baritone voice and sang in the church choir and a men's quartet, as well as performing as a guest soloist in community concerts such as *Elijah* or *Messiah*. Both he and Mom taught church school classes, Dad teaching high school boys (in our church, boys and girls attended different classes, as did men and women), and Mom taught an adult class. The earliest minister I can remember was George Johnson, a short but fiery Methodist preacher, who would shout and bang on the pulpit as a regular part of his sermons. One day, he made a pastoral call at our home and, in the course of the conversation, gave me a toy pistol. My mother was quite opposed to my having a gun, even a toy one, but because the minister gave it to me, she had little to say. As I look back on this, I think my mother was right, and I am happy to say that never in my ministry did I present a gun, toy or otherwise, to any of my parishioners!

At age fourteen, an event took place that immediately transferred me from a world where baseball was everything to a very different concern and pursuit. On October 4, 1957, the Soviet Union successfully launched the world's first satellite, *Sputnik I*. The event sent shock-waves throughout America and began the "space race." Throughout the country, public schools suddenly placed a high emphasis on science and mathematics. In my junior high school, some of us decided that singlehandedly, we would reverse the Soviet advantage and put America as number one again. (Yes, it was laughably presumptuous, but we were naïve enough to believe it.) We began constructing and launching homemade rockets—one boy in our school actually made a rocket that went out of sight. Of course, it did not go into orbit, but we had no idea where it came down. I began mixing chemicals in our basement (Mom did not sleep easily during those years), materials I obtained from a local pharmacist (today's pharmacists would undoubtedly be jailed if they provided chemicals to minors, especially those which could be explosive when combined). My school colleagues and I convinced a math teacher to instruct us in the most advanced form of technology we knew of, and in compliance with our request, he formed a Slide Rule Club. (This, too, is the stuff of pure comedy in a computer age, but I used that slide rule on a daily basis throughout high school and college. It was actually pretty sophisticated and could perform a number of arithmetic, logarithmic, and geometric functions.)

Upon graduation from high school, I was privileged to further my education at Cornell University, where for the first two years, I studied chemistry and physics, still intent on a career in science. I quickly discovered that chemistry, when seriously done, takes very hard work and is not nearly the fun and games I had imagined. Eight o'clock a.m. classes, where the lights were extinguished and the periodic table was projected onto a screen, became the occasion for a good nap. And memorizing the countless possibilities in organic chemistry was a chore I did not approach with joy. Qualitative analysis was the only course I found interesting and enjoyable. Physics, however, still captured my love and excitement.

I enjoyed the laboratory work and still remember the wise words of a professor who spoke English with a strong German accent: "Chust make certain you know vhat you are doing." It was a good lesson for life.

Another radical change in my life took place near the end of my sophomore year. A fraternity brother, Bob Shuman, participated in the Wesley Foundation, a Methodist group for college students. Bob was reading a book by the theologian Paul Tillich, *The Courage to Be*, and insisted—no, nagged is the better word—that I should read it too. I was not a regular part of the Wesley Foundation, but to get Bob off my back, I eventually gave in and purchased the book at the campus bookstore. It was a book I could not put down, a book that wrestled with questions with which I had been wrestling and that whet my appetite for theology. I began to seriously question if I was on the right career course. Confused and uncertain, I decided to spend that summer in thought about my life. I journeyed to Yellowstone National Park, where I worked in one of the park's service stations.

The trip west had several interesting experiences. I was as a passenger in a carload of three other young men from the college, heading westward. One was beginning grad school in Nebraska. When we were ready to depart, he climbed into the front passenger seat and deposited a large burlap bag between him and the driver. Not far into the trip the bag started moving. "What's in the bag?" our driver nervously asked. In response, the front-seat passenger opened the bag and pulled out two large king snakes. They were our traveling mates for well over a thousand miles. At night, we camped wherever we happened to be. The first night, somewhere in Missouri, we were swarmed by more mosquitoes than I have ever seen, and we hurried to throw up the tent, literally brushing mosquitoes off our bodies as we worked. The second night was by the side of the road between Laramie and Cheyenne. The night was clear and beautiful, so we decided not to pitch the tent. It is the only time I have slept on the ground, but it was a memorable experience, under a clear canopy of stars and listening to the howl of coyotes.

Arriving in Yellowstone, I spent two days in training in the town of Gardner, Montana, in a group of about thirty fellow summer employees. Then we were assigned to various service stations throughout the park. I dearly wanted to go to Old Faithful. Instead, I was the only one assigned to Fishing Bridge. It was disappointing, but either by sheer coincidence or by divine direction, it turned out to be a very significant assignment. The Hamilton Store next to the service station also hired seasonal college students, but unlike the service station, they included young women on their staff. One night, my colleagues and I held a "beach party," a bonfire on the sands of Yellowstone Lake. I invited a young woman from the "Hams" Store to go with me. She turned me down, since she already had a date. But pointing across the store, she informed me of the presence of a new employee who had just arrived and suggested that I invite her. Wow! What an incredibly beautiful young woman came into view! I invited her to go with me, and by incredibly good fortune or the grace of God, she agreed. She was a young woman from a small Montana town not far from the Northeast Entrance of Yellowstone, Mary Kay Cammack. We dated throughout that summer, if sitting on the Fishing Bridge in the late evenings after work and spending long hours in conversation can be considered dating. I spent the following Christmas with her family in her home, and we spent the next two summers together, the first at my home in Baltimore (where I worked as an electrician's helper, and she worked as a waitress in a White Coffee Pot Restaurant); the second in Minneapolis, where she was employed at Swedish Hospital, and I worked in a union job at a steel tubing mill. The following summer, on June 18, 1966, we married in First Nazarene Church in Billings.

Throughout that Yellowstone experience, I prayed for guidance for my life work, took long meditative hikes, and began to seriously read the Bible for the first time in my life. Vivid in my memory is a humorous story. One day, I sat behind the gas station, smoking a cigar, and reading the Bible. A fellow service station attendant, John Davis, happened to come by and asked me what I was doing. I told him I was reading the Bible. He asked why. For the first time, without thought and certainly without previously articulated intention, I answered, "I'm thinking about becoming a minister." And John Davis laughed and laughed; it was the craziest thing he had ever heard. Who knows but what John may well have been right.

Returning to Cornell, I had an immediate consultation with my advisor to share my unresolved thinking. Professor French (I don't know or remember his first name) gave me great advice, which is good advice for any undergraduate: expand your selection of courses. He encouraged me to take Greek and Roman history and especially to take a course in nineteenth-century American literature. At the time a course in nineteenth-century American literature was the last thing I would have wanted to study. Reluctantly, I followed his advice; after all, he was the advisor and I was the student. As I began to read the works of Nathaniel Hawthorne and Herman Melville, I understood why this kindly advisor made his recommendation. For Hawthorne and Melville write profound theology in a fictional venue. Perhaps all theology must be expressed in metaphor, parable, and imagery. How else can finite creatures comprehend that which is beyond?

# Christmas

A god who is outside history cannot save us. We live within history; we sin and grow old and die within history, and we must be saved by a god who has entered into the historical process. As long as a god remains a distant figure in a far corner of the universe, that god cannot help us. A god who does not enter into and transform the events that form our human life, birth, living, and death is of no value to us. A god who does not become flesh cannot bring us to redemption.

Likewise, a god who is bound by history cannot save us. No human being—however wise, however powerful, however inventive—can deliver us from the inextricable powers that reign over our earthly lives: sin and death. Having "the Great" after your name does not bring salvation. Conquering nations does not bring salvation. Discovering marvelous new insights and producing wondrous new devices does not save us. A god who does not come from beyond history cannot give us life.

When we speak of Christmas, what we are saying is this: the infinite and eternal God, the Creator of heaven and earth, became human and dwelt among us (John 1:14). God could have forced us into submission with awesome power and might. Instead, God wanted to change us from within. God wanted to feel what we feel, to suffer what we suffer, to die as we die. God wanted to set us free from the powers that destroy life and lead to death. God wanted to teach us that love counts for more than all the glories of this passing world. And so God came among us.

He came as a child, born of a woman in a small town in Israel. He lay in the straw of a common and lowly stable. He ran in the village streets with other children. He played in the sawdust of his father's carpentry shop and held his mother's hand as she drew a pail of water from the well. He had friends, and he had enemies. He knew our human grief, breaking down and crying shamelessly by the grave of a friend (John 11:35). He suffered as we suffer and feared as we are fearful. Fully and completely human, he lived among us. *He* lived among us—*he* who set the earth on its course and set the stars in the sky, *he* lived among us. *He* lived a human life, died a human death, and was buried in a human tomb. In resurrection, *he* overcame the human condition from within a human life. And because *he* did, we have become a new creation (2 Corinthians 5:17).

The presence of God in this world will not be found in power and arrogance. It will not be found in riches and splendor. It will not be found in hardened hearts and self-driven agendas. The presence of God will be seen in humility, in love, and in self-giving. It will be seen in a manger, a blood-stained cross, and an empty tomb.

As long as the Christ remains a distant figure from an age long gone, he is of no value to us or anyone else. His saving power arises when he enters our lives, and we allow his way of love and peace, humility, and forgiveness to pervade our whole being and transform our style of living. Then we will know him to be the Savior, the living Lord, the Eternal One in our midst.

And Christmas will be more than merry. It will be blessed.

# The Stable

The narrative of the birth of Jesus is filled with vivid imagery (Luke 2:1–20). A stable—crude and rustic, weathered under a Palestinian sun, its thatched roof dried and deteriorating. A mound of straw, a manger (not a cradle for a child but a feeding trough), an oil lamp hanging from a wooden peg, cobwebs in the dusty eaves. The smells, too, are coarse and earthy—some mold among the fodder and urine in the straw. And of course, there were the animals—perhaps a donkey, a cow, some sheep or goats, a mouse scurrying along the dirt floor. Such was the birthplace of the Savior.

There are some who say that animals came to see the newborn Messiah and, like the shepherds, offered their own form of worship and praise. But that is not correct.

The animals did not come to Jesus.

Jesus came to them.

The Lord of life came into their home, breathed his first breath in their stable, slept in their feeding trough, and lay his head on their straw.

And so it will come to be that the wolf shall lie down in peace with the lamb, the lion and calf together (Isaiah 11:6), and this whole fallen creation will be set free from death and will share in the glorious freedom of the sons and daughters of God (Romans 8:21).

Even a mouse on a stable floor.

# Pleasure and Joy

Christmas is a time of pleasure. Pleasures may be found everywhere: laughter-filled office parties; striking decorations of red and green, gold and silver; colorful packages adorned with ribbons and bows; and of course, "I'll Be Home for Christmas" playing in every elevator and shopping mall. From the child sitting on Santa's knee, wishing for a long list of games and toys, to the mature adult grazing at a holiday table filled with gourmet appetizers, nutmeg-sprinkled eggnog, and rich chocolates, Christmas abounds in pleasure.

But there is not pleasure for all. For at Christmas, like any other time of year, hospitals, hospices, and asylums are filled with suffering humanity. At Christmas, too, armies are on the move, bombs explode, and city streets are marred by crimes and murders. And yes, at this time of year also, children go without their daily bread, homeless sleep on park benches, and addicts lie in a stupor. For those who are still in grief, Christmas is especially painful, for there will be an empty place at the family table and a lonely aching in the heart. No wonder that churches provide "Blue Christmas" worship services, specifically targeted at all the people for whom there is no pleasure in Christmas.

Pleasure is not enough. No matter how much pleasure there is, it is not enough. What is desperately needed is more than pleasure. What is needed is joy.

Pleasure and joy are not the same. Pleasure remains on the surface, a passing gratification; joy has depth and fulfillment. Pleasure is found in escape from the problems of life; joy may be experienced in the midst of troubles. Pleasure is empty and hollow; joy is profound and lasting.

Can there be any joy—a real joy, a forever joy—or is a blissful and temporary pleasure all that can be reasonably expected? Is there a joy that is not offset by a corresponding sadness? Is there a hope that is more than an idle wish, an expectation that will be fulfilled? Is there a life that is not obliterated by death?

The message of Christmas is, above all, a message of joy. The joy of Christmas means that despite the defeats and disappointments of life, "all things work together for good for those who love God, who are called according to His purpose" (Romans 8:28). The joy of Christmas means that suffering, sorrow, pain, and death cannot prevent us from attaining the ultimate purpose and meaning of our existence. The joy of Christmas means that despite the sin and evil of humankind, there is a saving possibility in every situation, for nothing is outside the steadfast and eternal love of God.

At Christmas, something took place in human history that transforms the world. Something happened in time and space that overcomes the limits of time and space. Something happened in the old creation that ushers in a new creation. A light began to shine in the darkness, and all the darkness could not put it out (John 1:5). What has happened? What has happened is the birth of a child Emmanuel, God with us (Matthew 1:23). What has happened is that the eternal and sovereign God, the Creator of heaven and earth, has become incarnate in a human life. What has happened is that there is "good news of a great joy for all the people: to you is born this day in the city of David a Savior, who is the Messiah, the Lord" (Luke 2:10–11). What has happened is that "the Word became flesh and dwelt among us, full of grace and truth" (John 1:14).

Think what this means for the terminal cancer patient, languishing on a bed of pain. Think what it means for one standing by the grave of a dearest friend or family member. Think what it means for those at the end of their ropes, despondent and in despair. Think what it means for a world where all living creatures are under the curse of sin and death.

God has entered into our human existence. God knows what it is like to be worried and anxious. God knows what it is like to suffer, to grieve, and to be in pain. God knows what it is like to die and to be buried in a tomb. God himself has experienced it from within a human life, and God has overcome it from within a human life. As the early church teachers once affirmed, what God has assumed, God has redeemed. And what God has redeemed is our human life. God became human that that the human could become divine.

God knows what it is like—been there, done that. That is the message of Christmas.

And in that message, there is joy.

# Seeing God

"Whoever has seen me has seen the Father" (John 14:9).

Scarcely can I grasp the meaning of this text.

When I see Jesus, I see a gentle shepherd, caring for the flock, tenderly holding a lamb in his arms (John 10:11). To see that is to see the Father. That I can understand.

When I see Jesus, I see a wise teacher, calling on humankind to follow the ways of integrity and goodness (Matthew 5–7). To see that is to see the Father. That I can understand.

When I see Jesus, I see an angry man with a whip in his hand, driving thieves and oppressors from the temple courtyard (John 2:15). To see that is to see the Father, who will not tolerate injustice. That I can understand.

When I see Jesus, I see one who forgives an adulterous woman (John 8:3–10), one who heals the lame and the blind (Matthew 4:23), one who eats with tax collectors and sinners (Luke 15:1–2), one who calms the surging storms of life (Mark 4:35–39), and yes, even one who has the power and authority to raise the dead (John 11:17–44). To see that is to see the Father. And that too I can understand.

But when I see Jesus, I see something else, so shocking and unexpected that it goes beyond all my comprehension. I see a man whose hair is matted in blood, with spit on his beard and bruises on his cheeks, whose back has been reduced to a pulpy mess by the scourge, in whose hands and feet sharp spikes have been driven, and whose side has been split open with the thrust of a spear (John 19:1–37).

What if Jesus had not died? That, in effect, would be God saying, "I don't love you that much. I can't go that far. I will love you up to a point but no further." It would be God expressing the bottom-line truth of my life: "You are not worth dying for." But God does not say any of those things.

Love is not detached, it is not withdrawn, and it is not insulated from pain and suffering. That would be a contradiction of love. Love is not generic, vague, or theoretical. It is specific, tangible, and down-to-earth. Love that is not specific is not love at all. And never was the love of God more real, more clearly demonstrated, more direct and more certain than when, in excruciating pain, a man dropped his head and breathed his last (John 19:30). And he did it for me.

To see that is to see the Father.

# ✦ The Spring

Cold, even on the hottest of days, and clear, even on the murkiest of days, it comes flowing, gushing, and bursting forth. A spring supplies pure, fresh, life-giving water in constant and non-ending abundance.

Christ is like a spring of water. Not a glass of water. Not a pitcher of water. Not even a well of water. For those things can all be depleted and run dry. Christ is like a spring of water, bubbling forth in a never-ending supply of new life. "Those who drink of the water that I will give will never be thirsty. The water that I will give them will become in them a spring of water gushing up to eternal life" (John 4:14).

We need to hear and trust that image. For in this world, the demands and the needs and the pressures can be great and overwhelming. We may feel dried up and depleted. We may feel drained. We have been pushed to the limit, driven to the brink. We need to forgive, but we think we cannot forgive any more, for we have forgiven so much already. We need to give, but the needs are so great, and our time and money are exhausted. We are afraid to give any more. We need to love, but we feel empty and abused, too worn out to keep on loving. Have you not literally felt this way, drained and depleted by the problems of life? If you, the reader, have felt this way, these words are directed specifically toward you.

The problem is that we are drawing on a finite source. We are going to a well that can dry up, that can become weak, that can grow old, and that can become stagnant with despair. We are drawing upon our own resources. But we could be drawing from an infinite source. We could be drawing from a spring that gushes forth with strength and grace. We could be drawing from the infinite power that is available to us, the infinite power of God in Jesus Christ. Do not be afraid to draw upon that spring. Do not think for a minute that this source will dry up. It will not. It cannot. It will gush forth with an unending supply of living water.

When I rely upon my own resources, I am the weakest. When I rely upon the grace of the living God, I find strength and hope and power.

Do not turn to that which passes away, to that which grows weak and old, to that which can be used up. Wait on the One who can renew your strength like an eagle and in whose power you can run and not be weary; you can walk and not faint (Isaiah 40:31).

Listen! Even now, do you not hear it—the bubbling, the bursting, the gushing forth?

It is the spring of Christ.

And it is available for all.

# ✦ Ethics from the Future

Much of the time, our attitudes and behavior are based on things that have happened in the past.

Someone has offended us, hurt us, betrayed us, deceived us, or transgressed upon us in any of countless ways, big or small, real or perceived. We rage within, hold a grudge, speak ill of the perpetrator, or perhaps even actively seek vengeance. Our reaction is based on the past.

Nations, races, and cultures also act from the past. Injustices of hundreds of years ago live on; pride and the stubborn refusal to let go keep fires aflame and battles going. Murders, destruction, and wars are justified in the pretense of doing right and even claiming to be a directive of God. In Northern Ireland, a battle in 1689 causes contemporary troubles. In the Muslim world, a struggle for succession following the death of Muhammad, fourteen hundred years ago, causes Sunnis to bomb Shiites and Shiites to terrorize Sunnis. And in America, racial prejudices and divides have persisted, even a century and a half after the Civil War. Truly, the sins of the fathers are handed down to the third and fourth generation (Deuteronomy 5:9).

The ethics of Jesus look not to the past but to the future. Our attitudes and behavior must be based on what will happen, not on what has happened; on what will take place, not on what has taken place.

What will take place? In this world, we know not what a day may bring forth. But we do know something that most assuredly will take place. Jesus calls it the kingdom of God. God's sovereign reign over all things and over all persons will come into being, in God's good time and in God's good way. In that sovereign reign, there will be no evil, no hatred, no revenge, no bitterness, no getting even, no keeping score. There will be only love. The wrongs of the past will be no more.

The good news that Jesus proclaimed is that the kingdom of God is at hand (Mark 1:15) and that it is in your midst (Luke 17:21).

To say that God's kingdom is at hand is to say that we can reach out and touch it, that we can be part of it even now. It is already available to those who live in its glorious reality. Our behavior and our attitudes can be based on God's sovereign rule, which is coming and will be fulfilled.

God's kingdom will take place. If we have any sense at all, we shall form our ethical decisions on what will be and not on what will be no more.

# Out of Order

Surely he cannot be serious. Either this is some kind of a sick joke, or the man is completely out of his mind. "Love your enemies, do good to those who hate you, bless those who curse you, pray for those who abuse you" (Luke 6:27–28). Who would be so mentally unbalanced as to make that kind of a demand? Is Jesus a crazed lunatic? That is precisely the assumption made by his family when they came to "restrain" him, for people were saying, "He has gone out of his mind" (Mark 3:21). Get a grip, Jesus. You have been working too hard. Come on home and take a rest.

But if we conclude that Jesus has gone mad, we have drawn the wrong conclusion. It is not Jesus who is crazy; it is the world. It is a fallen world that seeks revenge, that wants to even the score, that readily practices an eye for an eye, and that resorts to violence as a means of solving disputes. It is a hardened heart that refuses to forgive, that keeps rehearsing anger, and that refuses to let go of even the slightest insult.

What is madness? Is it to love the neighbor, or is it to insist on a society where everyone carries their own automatic weapon? Is to seek transformation of broken lives, or is it to stone to death an adulterous woman? Is it to be a peacemaker, or is it to keep the fires of a nation's resentment burning for generation after generation? Is it to model bigotry and intolerance before children so they may live in the same tensions and terrors that we have known?

When a public toilet is not functioning properly, a sign is placed on the door: Out of Order. It is the world that needs a large sign, Out of Order, for to continue with the same hatreds, prejudices, deceptions, and retaliations is surely a disordered and destructive behavior.

There is a pronounced contradiction between the teachings of Jesus and the ways of the world. Jesus' commands are radical and culture-defying. But what would happen if God's children of every race and belief would actually "do unto others what you would have others do unto you" (Luke 6:31)? What would happen if the peoples of this planet really would love one another, and forgive one another, and speak the truth to one another, and be merciful to one another?

Jesus is not kidding. He is absolutely serious. To the neighbor who drives you crazy, to the son or daughter who rebels against your wishes, to the husband or wife who has failed you in so many ways, to the office colleague who has betrayed confidence or broken trust, to the insensitive friend who has hurt you with a demeaning attitude, and to all the others who harm and offend and perhaps have done so repeatedly, we are commanded to respond with love, forgiveness, and compassion.

The world cannot abide crazy people. We send them to asylums, lock them behind closed doors, and remove them from the public eye. Sometimes, we even burn them at the stake. One man was so deranged that he was beaten, stripped, and nailed to a cross. He was truly out of order.

Or was he?

#  No More!

"Put away from you all bitterness and wrath and anger and wrangling and slander, together with all malice, and be kind to one another, tenderhearted, forgiving one another, as God in Christ has forgiven you" (Ephesians 4:31–32).

We might assume that these words were written to two angry gangs, ready to fight it out with knives and chains on the streets of the inner city. Or we might think that these words were addressed to close-minded politicians, heatedly bickering over a partisan issue, and in so doing, losing all respect from the general public. But these words were not specifically targeted at them. No more bitterness, no more wrath, no more anger, no more wrangling, no more slander, no more malice—these words were addressed to a Christian church.

Sadly, we must confess that bigotry, intolerance, and hatred have, like an insidious poison, infected the Christian Church, not only in Ephesus of the first century AD but in all times and in all places. Throughout the centuries, the church has been divided against itself, torn by schism, divisiveness, and prejudice. Even today, petrol bombs are thrown in Belfast by both fanatic Protestants and Catholics. It is an embarrassment to people of faith and a grievous offense against the Prince of Peace. No more!

Peaceful unity in the church is not an option. It is not a luxury to enjoy or do without. It is not to be treated lightly or ignored. It is God's will that his people be one. When Jesus prayed in Gethsemane, the night before his crucifixion, he prayed for his disciples, and he also prayed "on behalf of those who will believe in me through their word, that they may all be one" (John 17:20–21). That they may *all* be one. That they may all be *one*.

Peaceful unity is not based on our opinions. It is not based on our particular interpretation of Scripture or doctrine. It is not based on a proud assertion of the rightness of our denomination, or the foolish notion that our group has all the truth and others are in some way corrupt. Our unity is based on Christ, who forgives all, loves all, and unites us all in his one body.

Peaceful unity is not just a theological concern. It is very much a practical matter. We live in a world of hunger, of sickness and disease, and of unchecked human need. A divided church cannot meet those needs. And we live in a world of disbelief and doubt. Well, no wonder!

Why would a nonbeliever want to be part of a church that is broken by dissension and conflict? For the sake of every starving child, for the sake of every grieving mourner, for the sake of every confused teenager, for the sake of every skeptic, from the casual "none" to the most hardened anti-theist, the church must be one.

The very first Sunday school lesson that I can remember, back when I was in a nursery class in the days after the most death-dealing war in human history, was a little song. How tragic when we forget what is possibly the most basic and fundamental teaching of our faith. "Jesus loves the little children, all the children of the world. Red and yellow, black and white, they are precious in his sight, for he loves the little children of the world."

What is needed? The divided church in Ephesus was given the answer:

"Lead a life worthy of the calling to which you have been called, with all humility and gentleness, with patience, bearing with one another in love, making every effort to maintain the unity of the Spirit, in the bond of peace" (Ephesians 4:1–3).

Humility is needed, for we all need to be forgiven. Gentleness is needed, for every person is a precious child of God. Patience is needed, for our differences can be a strength and not a weakness. God loves us in our differences, and our differences are transcended in his truth.

To all my Christian brothers and sisters, I say, "No more!" No more division! No more intolerance! No more conflict! Actually, it is not I who say it. It is the Lord.

No more means no more!

## Open Hands, Softened Hearts

A closed hand is a fist. A closed hand represents aggression and hostility; it can be used like a weapon to hurt and bring harm. A closed hand represents grabbing, holding tight, and grasping something for oneself.

An open hand is a very different image. An open hand can be used to shake hands with a friend or to meet a stranger. You cannot shake hands with a closed fist. An open hand can give an encouraging pat on the back, to reach out in an embrace, or to wave a warm hello to someone passing by. An open hand can give. And an open hand can receive.

God asks for open hands. The God of infinite and inexhaustible blessings is pleased when we openly and thankfully receive his gifts. And God demands that we do not close our hands or harden our hearts to neighbors in need. "You shall not harden your heart or shut your hand against your poor brother, but you shall open your hand to him, and lend him sufficient for his need, whatever it may be. … Since there will never cease to be someone in need on the earth, I therefore command you, 'Open your hand to the poor and needy neighbor in your land'" (Deuteronomy 15:7–8, 11).

The hardened heart, the "heart of stone," as Ezekiel called it (Ezekiel 36:26), is the symbol of a proud and callous attitude, an attitude that is self-centered and arrogant. There are many subtle ways to have a hardened heart, ways used to justify a failure to help. The poor are lazy; they refuse to work; they are here illegally; they have no motivation; they are alcoholics; they are on drugs. How clever we are in creating excuses not to help! But even helping, with a hardened heart, such as when I might drop some coins in a beggar's cup simply to get rid of him, is of little value. The softened heart is gracious, gentle, and compassionate. It is sensitive to need without being judgmental. It offers assistance with gladness. Both the open hand and the softened heart are needed. It does no good to give with a grudge. And it does no good to have a sentimental thought about the poor without an open hand to go with it.

Let there be no mistake: this is the command of the sovereign God, the Alpha and Omega of all that is. It is not just a sweet little humanitarian gesture. It is a religious obligation. It is the logical consequence of that fundamental religious principle: "You shall love the Lord your God with all your heart, and with all your soul, and with all your mind, and with all your strength, and you shall love your neighbor as yourself" (Mark 12:30–31). (The old rabbis interpreted "strength" to mean not our physical strength but our material wealth and assets.)

In the fourth century, there lived a man named Martin of Tours. He became the patron saint of France. He is to France what Patrick is to Ireland. Martin was a soldier in the Roman army, serving in what was then called Gaul. He was not a wealthy man and lived simply on a soldier's pay. One day, Martin encountered a beggar. It was the dead of winter, bitter cold, and with a penetrating wind. The beggar was shivering. Martin had no money. All he had was his soldier's cloak, which was worn and frayed. He took it off, cut it in half with his sword, and gave half to the beggar and then continued on his way.

That night, Martin had a dream, or perhaps it was a vision. Martin saw the heavenly kingdom and all the angels in their glory. In the midst of the scene, there was Jesus, draped in half of a Roman soldier's cloak. One of the angels asked, "Lord, why are you wearing that half-cloak?" And Jesus answered, "Martin gave it to me."

Is it too inconceivable to comprehend that one day, in a kingdom far more glorious and wonderful than we have ever known, that we might encounter a familiar face, a friendly figure carrying a warm coat, or blanket, or bowl of rice, or vial of medicine, or simply a cup of cold water? And when the angels ask him, Lord, why are you holding that?, he might simply answer, _____ gave it to me. (Fill in your own name in the blank.)

Whatever we have done to the least of his brothers and sisters, we have done to the Lord (Matthew 25:40).

Unclench your fist. Open your hand. And smile.

## Only Two

We live in a troubling and disturbing world. Natural disasters can strike at any time, destroying lives, homes, and property. Terrorists plant bombs that take the lives of innocent people, and then, even more insidiously, plant devices triggered to detonate as rescue workers arrive to help the bloodied victims. Hunger, disease, and illiteracy abound, and shelters and refugee camps are filled with homeless people. Wars and rumors of wars have not ceased (Matthew 24:6). It is a troubling and disturbing world.

To this troubling and disturbing world, Jesus speaks troubling and disturbing words. He tells of the final judgment, when all nations will be gathered before the Son of Man (Matthew 25:31–46).

The blessed will be welcomed into a kingdom of joy and peace:

> 'I was hungry and you gave me food, I was thirsty and you gave me drink, I was a stranger and you welcomed me, I was naked and you gave me clothing, I was sick and you took care of me, I was in prison and you visited me.' Then the righteous will answer him, 'Lord, when was it that we saw you hungry and gave you food, or thirsty and gave you something to drink? And when was it that we saw you a stranger and welcomed you, or naked and gave you clothing? And when was it that saw you sick or in prison and visited you?' And the king will answer them, 'Truly, I tell you, just as you did it to one of the least of these who are members of my family, you did it to me' (Matthew 25:35–40).

The cursed will be condemned to eternal fire:

> 'I was hungry and you gave me no food, I was thirsty and you gave me nothing to drink, I was a stranger and you did not welcome me, naked and you did not give me clothing, sick and in prison and you did not visit me.' Then they will also answer, 'Lord, when was it that we saw you hungry or thirsty or a stranger or naked, or sick or in prison, and did not take care of you?' Then he will answer them, 'Truly I tell you, just as you did not do it to one of the least of these, you did not do it to me' (Matthew 25:42–45).

Do not assume that it is just a parable. Many of Jesus' parables begin with the key word "like": "The kingdom of heaven is like a mustard seed ..." (Matthew 13:31), or "The kingdom of heaven is like a treasure hidden in a field ..." (Matthew 13:44). But there is no "like" to introduce these words. Rather, Jesus said, "When the Son of Man comes in his glory ..."(Matthew 25:31). When—not "if," not "maybe," but "when." It is not a parable. It is a glimpse of what will be.

There are only two kingdoms. In this world there are many kingdoms, dominions, empires, and caliphates that rise and fall. But ultimately, there are only two. One is a kingdom of light; the other of darkness. One is a realm of joyful giving; the other is a realm of self-serving greed. One is filled with trusting confidence in the living God; the other is full of fretful worry and discontent. One is lived in the presence of God; the other is marred by separation and estrangement. There are only two kingdoms. Every act that we do, every word that we speak, every thought that we harbor advances the cause of one of those two kingdoms. Every step that we take moves us closer to an eternal destiny in the kingdom of God or in the kingdom of death.

What leads us to those kingdoms? What distinguishes the occupants of these two realms? Surprisingly, nothing is said about attending church, or going to Bible study, or saying your prayers. Perhaps those things are assumed. What matters is whether you love your neighbor, whether you feed the hungry, offer a cold drink to the thirsty, welcome the stranger, clothe the naked, and visit the sick and the imprisoned. The difference is love! To love the neighbor is to love the Lord himself.

There are two choices before us: to give or not to give. To care or not to care. To serve or not to serve. To love even the least of his brothers or sisters or not to love.

Please do not assume that there are other choices. There are not.

There are only two.

# The Test

Thomas put Jesus to the test. After Jesus was raised from the dead, Thomas said, "Unless I see the mark of the nails in his hands, and put my fingers in the mark of the nails and my hand in his side, I will not believe" (John 20:25).

Jesus showed Thomas the marks in his hands. "Have you believed because you have seen me? Blessed are those who have not seen and yet have come to believe" (John 20:29).

Jesus passed the test. He really had died. He really had been raised. His hands gave visible proof that he was the resurrected Lord.

But what if Jesus turned the test around? What if Jesus asked to see your hands? What if Jesus said, "I want to see your hands. I don't want to see hands that are soft, smooth, and pampered. I don't want to see hands that are moistened by rich and luxurious lotions. I don't want to see hands that reflect a life of ease and comfort and indolence. I want to see hands that have some dirt under the fingernails. I want to see hands that are nicked and stained. I want to see hands that have some scars."

What if Jesus said, "I want to see hands that prove you are my disciple"? "I want to see hands that have served food in a homeless shelter, hands that have known the dust of drywall in a Habitat for Humanity dwelling, hands that are soiled from changing diapers in a church nursery, hands that are chapped from raking leaves or shoveling snow for an elderly neighbor, hands that have reached out to touch a prisoner or welcome a stranger, hands that are wearied and swollen from deeds of loving kindness."

The good news of saving grace is also a summons to a new life. It is a call to love one another, to work for justice for the downtrodden, to seek peace when others are calling for blood, to give and to serve. It is dying to self and being raised with Christ. It is being transformed into his glorious likeness. It means rolled-up sleeves and dirty hands.

Show me your hands.

Jesus passed the test.

Will you?

#  The Mirror

If I look into a mirror, I see an image of myself reflected back.

Human lives are created in the image of God. "So God created man in his own image, in the image of God He created him; male and female He created them" (Genesis 1:27). This does not mean that we are miniature reproductions of God or that God looks like one of us, blown up really big. It means that we are created to be mirrors, to reflect back the image of God. We are created to reflect God's love, God's goodness, and God's compassion. More than that, we are made to reflect God's justice, seeking what is right and what is fair. More than that, we are to reflect God's rationality, praising the Creator of a rational universe that, quite amazingly, is open to being rationally understood by humans. God is to be imaged in us, in the way we live, in the way we love, in the way we forgive, in our thoughts, in our attitudes, in our words, and in our deeds.

Now, if a mirror is tilted away from the one who looks in it, that person does not see his or her own image reflected back. He or she may see the floor, or the ceiling, or perhaps a wall. The tragic reality of human life is that we are tilted away from being aligned with the Creator, and when God looks upon us, he sees only flawed and sinful individuals. Instead of love, God sees self-centeredness. Instead of justice, God sees bloodshed. Instead of rationality, God sees a rejection of both faith and reason in those who would reduce a beautiful, intricate, and finely tuned universe to only matter and energy.

God did not make the world the way a carpenter would make a table or a chair, an object apart from himself. When God brought forth the universe, he did so with a word. "God said, Let there be light, and there was light" (Genesis 1:3). "He spoke, and it came to be; he commanded, and it stood forth" (Psalms 33:9). God spoke with the voice of one who is involved, who wants to be in communication with his creation. God speaks. Our job is to listen, to answer, to live in relationship, and to remember we are his creatures, made to be his image.

It is one of the commandments that we are not to make a graven image of God (Exodus 20:4).

We are that image.

The mirror of our lives is created to reflect back God.

# The Changed Sentence

Who did it? Somebody changed the sentence.

Remember the old children's game in which a sentence is passed around the room from child to child? One child begins the game by whispering a sentence into the ear of another child. That child whispers the sentence into the ear of yet another, and so it goes around the room. Often, the sentence is at least slightly distorted by the time it gets to the last child. Everyone wonders, who changed it? And why?

Somebody changed the sentence. And I suspect that it was intentionally changed. You see, this sentence wasn't just a sentence in a children's game, like "The red cow is in the old brown barn." No, this sentence was a part of Holy Scripture. This sentence was divinely inspired, carefully handed down from generation to generation. Century after century, this sentence had been passed on, unchanged. And somebody changed it. And we know who did it. It was Jesus who made the change.

In the book of Leviticus, part of the Torah of the people of the Hebrew people, there is a fundamental and basic commandment: "You shall be holy, for I the Lord your God am holy" (Leviticus 19:2). You are to be holy because God is holy. That is not something to be taken lightly. It is to be rigorously and faithfully observed.

And Jesus changed it. "Be merciful even as your Father is merciful" (Luke 6:36). You are to be merciful. You are to be compassionate. You are to be caring and loving, even as God is caring and loving. To be merciful as the Father is merciful is to love with a steadfast love, an unfailing love, and an unconditional love, a love that is constant and faithful no matter what.

No doubt God wants us to be holy. But if Jesus is right, God's main concern is that we be merciful. That's "job one" for God.

Get rid of all bitterness, all scorn, all contempt, all hatred, all prejudice, and all the vengeful ill will that may be lurking deep down inside. Leave it behind and move on. Give freely, serve freely, and forgive freely. Let your heart be filled with love, compassion, and mercy.

Because somebody changed the sentence.

Love is God's top priority. And you cannot be holy unless you love.

# ✺ All by Grace

Two men came to the temple to pray. One of them was a Pharisee, a very good man. His whole life was a model of righteousness. He never swindled anyone out of anything. All his business dealings were honest and just. He never cheated on his wife, and he was patient with his children. Not only was he a good man, but he also was a religious man. He faithfully attended the synagogue worship and spent long hours in study of the Torah. He fasted twice a week and meticulously tithed of his substance. He genuinely was a good man. He lifted his prayer to God, and God, in effect, answered, "Yeah, yeah, I don't want to hear about it."

The other man who prayed was a dirty, lowdown scoundrel. He was a thief of the worst kind. He became wealthy by cheating people, skimming off everything he could bleed out of them. And all the while, he was collaborating with the enemy, collecting taxes for an oppressive Roman government. He was the lowest of the low. He, too, prayed at the temple, and he returned to his home, buddy-buddy with God.

This story, related by Luke (Luke 18:9–14), is shocking. More than shocking, it is outrageous. Are we to believe that the good, religious man is rejected by God, while the despicable sinner was welcomed with open arms? No wonder the religious leaders decided to crucify Jesus, who went around telling stories like this.

Perhaps there is more to the story.

The Pharisee, for all his goodness and religiosity, was filled with pride and self-righteousness: "God, I thank you that I am not like other people: thieves, rogues, adulterers, or even like this tax collector. I fast twice a week; I give a tenth of all my income" (Luke 18:11–12). I am not like others. I fast. I tithe. That's a lot of I's. It is precisely that kind of self-sufficiency and self-centeredness that cuts us off from God and from others as well. What is this man's standard anyway? Is it the tax collector? By that standard, the Pharisee might rightly think, *I have my faults, but I am considerably better than this little creep.* But what if the standard is the holy righteousness of God? By that standard, he is a poor and dying sinner, desperately in need of grace.

All sin is dangerous. All sin is destructive and undermining. But the most self-threatening sin of all is the attitude that we do not need God, that we can get along very well on our own. The Pharisee failed to realize that it is all by grace. It is only by grace that any of us woke up this morning. It is only by grace that we have anything that we have. It is only by grace that any prayer is possible. It is only by grace that we have life. And it is only by grace that we have the hope of eternal life.

The tax collector knew how much he needed God. He understood that apart from God's grace, he was lost. He realized that he needed to be rescued from sin and death, that he needed a Savior. He came before God, simply asking for mercy, and mercy was freely given.

Both the Pharisee and the tax collector were sinners. One sinned by blatant wickedness, the other by an arrogant failure to love. Both broke the Father's heart; both fell short of God's intention for their lives. One received grace; the other felt that he did not need it. Both heaven and hell are made up of sinners. Those in heaven have accepted forgiveness. Those in hell think that they do not need it.

But here is the real truth of Jesus' parable. Both the Pharisee and the tax collector are part of us. They are not fictional characters of two thousand years ago but accurate descriptions of our own attitudes and behaviors. They live deep down inside Everyman and Everywoman. We all have the capacity to be self-reliant and ignore the grace that is offered. And we all have the capacity to forgive and be forgiven, and in so doing, to be reconciled to God and to others.

Put out of your mind all the reasons why you think God should be honored to have you enter his kingdom. Put out of your mind all the accomplishments and achievements that you think make you better than your neighbor. Put out of your mind all the money you have ever earned and all the assets you have set aside to guarantee your security. Put out of your mind all the good deeds you have ever done. Stop trying to justify yourself before God. Just accept grace. Nothing more. Nothing less. Just accept that in Jesus Christ, the living God loves you, and accepts you, and forgives you, and wants you to live with him forever.

For here is what we rely upon. The One who gives sight to the blind and makes the lame to walk, the One who raises the dead and calms the stormy sea, the One who feeds the multitude and proclaims good news to the poor, and the One who is the Alpha and Omega of all that is also is the One who is a friend of tax collectors and sinners, and yes, the friend of self-righteous Pharisees who will open their hearts to his grace.

It is all by grace.

It is all by grace.

##  Forgetful

How would one describe God? There are many adjectives we might use. Our God is almighty, eternal, all-knowing, all-powerful, and immortal. God is all this and more. But there is one that must be added to the list, one that is essential to the very nature and character of the deity. God is forgetful. Yes, our God is forgetful, as forgetful as an old man who cannot remember if he took his blood pressure medicine—indeed, he cannot even remember if he had his breakfast.

Actually, it is not that God cannot remember. It is that God does not remember. God intentionally chooses *not* to remember: "I will forgive their iniquity, and remember their sin no more" (Jeremiah 31:34).

God remembers our sin no more! Picture the scene. There is sin that is eating away inside you, an unresolved guilt from years ago, or perhaps something that happened this past week. Something you said, or did, or failed to do caused deep hurt, broke a relationship, or created great trouble, and it is tearing you up inside. It is an ugly and sordid stain on your whole life; you live under the cloud of shame. Finally you get up the nerve to confess your sin to God. And God says, "You did that? That's funny; I don't remember."

"But God, I did it yesterday!"

"Really? I just don't remember."

The prophet Micah said that God will cast all our sins into the depths of the seas (Micah 7:19). And when they are cast into the depths of the sea, they are gone forever. "As far as the east is from the west, so far he removes our transgressions from us" (Psalm 103:12). We are forgiven! "Where sin increased, grace abounded all the more!" (Romans 5:20).

We need to take the good news of these biblical images seriously. When God forgives, God forgives completely. Our sin is no longer held against us. What this means is that the past—however unpleasant, however destructive—does not need to ruin our future. We are free from the past. We are free to lift our drooping heads. We are free to enjoy a new life, free to forgive others as we have been forgiven, free to love, free to be happy, and free to be at peace within ourselves.

If God forgives you, you need to forgive yourself. Otherwise, you are putting yourself above God. And that would be a violation of the very first commandment (Exodus 20:3).

What a wondrous God we serve. "Nothing will be impossible with God" (Luke 1:37). Our God is awesome. Our God is eternal. Our God is almighty. Our God is incredibly great.

And yes, thank God, our God is very forgetful.

# Religious?

Was Jesus a religious person?

The reader may immediately answer, Yes, you idiot, of course Jesus was religious. He was the foremost of religious persons. He was a man of prayer, a man filled with the Spirit, a man deeply and closely in touch with God—so close that he dared to make the claim that "whoever has seen me has seen the Father" (John 14:9), and "I and the Father are one" (John 10:30). He inspired and instituted one of the world's great religions. Of course Jesus was religious.

But suppose that question were asked of the Pharisees or scribes of Jesus' day, or to the high priests Annas and Caiaphas, or to the Sadducees. They would have answered, No, he was not religious. He broke the Sabbath, picking grains of wheat on the God-commanded day of rest. He and his disciples did not fast the way that religious people are supposed to fast. He ate and drank with tax-collectors and sinners. He repeatedly called the religious authorities "hypocrites," "fools," and "blind guides" (Matthew 23). He was the opposite of what religious people are supposed to be and do.

So was Jesus religious? It all depends on how you define religious. Is religion rigorous obedience to traditions, laws, rules, regulations, and customs? Is religion of matter of strictly fulfilling the legalistic requirements needed to appease judgmental leaders of a church, mosque, or synagogue? Or is religion what James said it was: "visiting orphans and widows in their affliction, and keeping oneself unstained from the world" (James 1:27)? Is religion what Amos understood when, speaking for God, he said, "I hate, I despise your feasts ... take away from me the noise of your songs ... but let justice roll down like waters and righteousness like an ever flowing stream" (Amos 5:24)?

Actually, it all depends on how we understand God. How does God define religion? What does God ask of religious people? Hosea, speaking for God, declares the answer: "I desire steadfast love, not sacrifice" (Hosea 6:6). *God* desires steadfast love, not sacrifice. God seems to have no interest in religious rituals, rules, and regulations. God wants us to be people of steadfast love, a love that is unconditional, constant and faithful, unchanging and undiminished. It is love embodied in a man on a cross, laying down his life for the world. Without steadfast love, all the religious traditions, all the religious customs, all the worship services, all the sermons, all the praise songs and hymns, all the catechisms and creeds, all the vestments and incense and candles—all of it—amount to nothing more than a pile of dung. Such religion is a sham and is rightfully renounced by the world's atheists.

The highest calling in life is not to be religious. It is to be like Christ. It is to follow him, to love like him, to forgive like him, to serve like him, and to trust like him. In doing so, we may or may not be religious. But we shall be the sons and daughters of God.

# ✦ Ugly

It was ugly, very ugly. Cheap, low, tacky, petty—yes, it was all of these and more. "A dispute arose among them, which of them was to be regarded as the greatest" (Luke 22:24). The disciples of Jesus were arguing among themselves as to who was the greatest. What makes their behavior even more despicable is the context in which the argument took place. It was the Last Supper of Jesus, his last supper upon this earth, the exemplary moment when he got down on his knees and washed the feet of the ones who would vainly argue. It was that shared and sacred meal wherein just as the bread was broken, so would his body be broken, and just as the wine was poured into the cup, so his blood would flow out from his hands, his feet, his thorn-crowned head, and his side. In that very moment the followers of Jesus were arguing about who would be the greatest. It was ugly all right, real ugly.

I, for one, am very glad that this story is in the Bible.

The story shouts of authenticity. If the Gospels were fabrications of Jesus' earliest followers, as some critics suggest, this story would not be there. If the life, death, and resurrection of Jesus were simply made-up stories, this event would not be in the Bible. The denial by Peter would not be there. The betrayal by Judas would not be there. The doubting of Thomas would not be there. If this were all a fabrication, surely the disciples would have made themselves look considerably better than the texts show them to be. This is not a fairy tale. This is the way it was, as squalid as degrading as it may be. This is real, a blunt and honest reflection of human pride.

More than authenticity, the story conveys good news. Jesus died for these disciples. Jesus died not for saints and holy heroes but for self-serving, self-righteous, self-centered sinners. And that means he died for me. He died for me and for all those who fret about who will have the most rewards, the biggest desk in the office, the flashiest car, the most fashionable clothing, the most prestigious wristwatch, or the largest home with the very finest waterfront view. He died for us, despite our petty sinfulness. He hung on the cross for us. He who was the incarnate God laid down his life for the healing of our lives.

Saving grace may be found in a sordid and ugly surrounding.

Sinful and selfish as I am, that is good news. It is very good news indeed.

# Angry

How could he be so angry? Things started out quite well. His disciples had done exactly as he had asked them do, going into the village and obtaining a donkey (Mark 11:2). He had ridden the donkey into the city of Jerusalem, surrounded by a large crowd of cheering people. They spread garments in his path and leafy branches on the roadway. They gave him the highest of accolades: "Blessed is the one who comes in the name of the Lord! Blessed is the coming kingdom of our ancestor David!" (Mark 11:9–10). For Jesus, the day was going very well.

He came to the temple, and here was his chance to solidify his support—shake a few hands, pat a few backs, socialize with the folks in power, be seen with all the right people. How could he ask for more? But his anger quickly flared. "And he entered the temple and began to drive out those who were selling and those who were buying in the temple, and he overturned the tables of the money changers, and the seats of those who sold doves …" (Mark 11:15).

Why the anger? What was the big deal? It was just business—and business as usual. Surely it was good for the economy, and if it was good for the economy, why not do it? And this was intense anger. He drove them out! That is a strong verb—drove. He drove them out, like you might drive out a herd of unruly cattle. John's Gospel says that he drove them out with a "whip of cords" (John 2:15). This does not sound like gentle Jesus. Driving people out of the temple with a whip is not the way to build your fan club, and it certainly does not fit the expected behavior of a Prince of Peace. You would have thought that he owned the temple.

Actually, he did own the temple! After all, isn't this guy supposed to be the incarnation of God? We humans get angry, and often say harsh words and react in irrational ways. But God is beyond our sinful natures. God is sheer goodness. How could God be angry?

Actually, the question is not, how could the Lord be angry? The question is, how could he not be angry? God's temple was being abused. But worse than that, God's people were being abused. They were being cheated, defrauded, and ripped off, and all in the name of religion. Dealers were overcharging, like hot-dog vendors in a sports stadium. Money changers were overcharging, like the exchange machines at an international airport. And they were selling sacrificial birds and animals, as if atonement for sin is something that can be purchased with money. The house of prayer for all had truly become a den of robbers (Mark 11:17).

Jesus not only drove out the sellers, but he also drove out the buyers. Could it be that the buyers are as guilty as the sellers? Is it not the demand to buy that allows the merchants of corruption to prosper? How many purveyors of pornography would stay in business if those of every religion who profess faith in a higher power would cease to purchase their products? How many casinos and lotteries would flourish if religious people would refrain from the lure of instant riches—riches gained without providing a good or service? How many prostitutes would ply their trade on our streets if people with at least some degree of faith would seek a relationship based on love and faithfulness? How many drug dealers would continue to promote their poison if youth or adults who came from religious homes would say, "No more."

Do we understand that every time we spend even so much as one dollar, we are making a moral decision? Money is a tool that can be used for good or for evil. It can be spent to enrich life in a positive way, or it can be spent to support a practice that destroys and dehumanizes. It can build up or it can tear down.

Jesus did not cleanse the temple because he hated it. He did so because he loved it. He did not drive out people because he wished them ill. He did so because he wanted to change them and lift them to a higher way of life. The one who overturned the tables wants to turn over our way of living.

He calls us to turn away from all deception, cheating, swindling, and stealing and to avoid all forms of exploitation. He calls us to a transformed life, a life that shares a coat with one who has none (Luke 3:11), forgives not seven times but seventy times seven times (Matthew 18:22), and loves the enemy, does good to those who hate you, blesses those who curse you, and prays for those who abuse you (Luke 6:27–28). It is a life that is grounded in the power of resurrection and eternal life. The cleansing of the temple teaches us that a God of love and justice demands love and justice from us.

Perhaps more than any other event, the cleansing of the temple led Jesus to the cross. Immediately after hearing of Jesus' angry act, the chief priests and scribes began looking for a way to kill him (Mark 11:18). When he drove out the buyers and sellers, Jesus was, in effect, signing his own death warrant. He did it for the sake of those very buyers and sellers. He did it for the priest and scribes who were plotting to kill him. He did it for the soldiers who pounded nails into his hands and feet. He did it for an unjust and fallen world. He did it for you. And he did it for me.

Thanks be to God that he was so angry.

## ❊ Remember This Night

It was a lovely spring night with a moonlit sky and a balmy breeze. My wife and I and a few friends were enjoying one of the privileges of living near Washington, DC. We were sitting on the west lawn of the capitol, listening to a concert by the National Symphony Orchestra. From where we sat, we could see in the distance the towering pillar of the Washington Monument, majestic in the moonlight. The sounds of violin and cello, trumpet and tuba embraced us, lifting mind and spirit.

At the end of the concert, as the crowd began to disperse, I overheard a mother speaking to her young child. She took the child by the hand and turned around to look at the capitol one last time. "Remember that sight," she said. "Remember that you have seen it." I assume that they were from out of the area, perhaps visiting Washington for the first time, perhaps the only time they would ever have this experience. She wanted her child to remember it.

I have been in downtown DC many times and thus take much for granted. I suddenly realized that this night was not to be taken for granted. This night was a precious experience. This night was worth remembering. The majestic marble dome—the symbol of freedom and democracy, of free speech and thought and religion, the emblem of a free people—gleamed in the floodlights against the darkness of the sky. The mother's words were good advice for me. "Remember that sight." Remember what it represents. Remember that you were there.

It was something like this that Jesus wanted to impress upon his disciples on the night of the Last Supper. They had gathered in an upper room to observe the Passover meal. Jesus wanted his followers to remember God's mighty act in delivering Israel from slavery. He wanted them to remember what Jews of every generation are asked to remember: "We were Pharaoh's slaves in Egypt, but the Lord brought us out of Egypt with a mighty hand" (Deuteronomy 6:21).

But Jesus wanted them to remember something else. Remember *this* night. Remember our journey over the dusty road from Bethany. Remember how I took a towel, stooped down, and washed your feet. Remember my example: "If I, your Lord and Teacher, have washed your feet, you also ought to wash one another's feet" (John 13:14). Remember how I broke the bread and lifted the cup of salvation. Remember what it signifies: my body, broken for you; my blood, shed for you and for many, for the forgiveness of sin. Let this night sink deeply into your minds, so that whenever you eat and drink, you will remember that I love you, that I gave myself for you, and that I offer you newness of life.

Eat bread. Drink wine. Wash feet.

Remember this night. It is worth remembering as long as you live.

# Too Short

Life is short. Life is very short. With vivid imagery, the psalmist reminds us of the brevity of all earthly life: "As for mortals, their days are like grass; they flourish like the flower of the field; for the wind passes over it and it is gone, and its place knows it no more" (Psalm 103:15–16).

Life is so short that it must determine the way we live.

Life is too short to work at a job you do not enjoy or that is not fulfilling.

Life is too short to sit indoors when the leaves of October are in full color, or the dogwood is blossoming in the springtime, or the crepe myrtle is blooming in midsummer.

Life is too short not to hang a bird feeder in the backyard and fill it with sunflower seeds and millet.

Life is too short not to take a bag of groceries to the local food closet or bring a sandwich and a cup of coffee to the homeless man who sleeps under the bridge.

Life is too short, as you come and go from your home each evening, not to look up at the stars.

Life is too short to make your bed every day.

Life is too short to eat yogurt when ice cream is being offered.

Life is too short not to go to a grandchild's soccer game and to joyfully say, "You played a good game," even when your team lost by a score of eight to nil.

Life is too short not to play in the surf at Ocean City at least once a season and to tour a foreign country at least once a lifetime.

Life is too short not to get up in the dark of night, to stand on a wind-chilled beach on Easter morning and, as the first rays of light brighten the far horizon, sing with all your heart, "Christ the Lord is risen today."

Life is too short not to lend a helping hand, not to speak a word of encouragement, not to be forgiving, not to fall on your knees and say, "Thank you."

Most of all, life is too short not to love. Without love, we are nothing.

For more than forty years, I was a Christian minister. And what do I have to commend myself? My earliest colleagues met in tombs. My first bishop was a fisherman. My heroes were beheaded or burned at the stake. My only hope rests on a carpenter who was crucified between two thieves. Ultimately, love is the only thing I have to give. And it is the only thing anyone has to give.

Life is too short not to give it.

## ❀ Third Diversion

Three questions must be answered in the course of our lives. If we answer any one of these three questions incorrectly, we will pay the price in misery and unhappiness:

Will I marry? (And if so, to whom?) What will be my work, my vocation (from *vocatio*, my calling)? To what or whom will I devote my life?

By grace and by no skill or wisdom of my own, I answered these questions in the right way for my life.

On June 18, 1966, in a Nazarene church in Billings, Montana, Mary Kay Cammack and I were united in marriage. For me, the ancient description of marriage came true: Mary Kay is "bone of my bone and flesh of my flesh" (Genesis 2:23), and my life has been immensely blessed in our marriage. To be sure, there have been arguments and challenging times, for so it will be when any two persons endeavor to live and partner together. But our wedded life has been enriched by a steadfast and unconditional love that has given us much joy and fulfillment.

Our marriage began in Edinburgh, Scotland, where I spent the second year of my theological school training. Edinburgh was fortunate to escape heavy bombing in World War II and in many ways maintains the look and spirit of a medieval European city. New College, the seminary of the University of Edinburgh, is located by the Royal Mile, the long street sloping from the castle, past St. Giles' Cathedral and the home of John Knox, to Holyrood Palace, the home of monarchy from the days of Mary, Queen of Scots. Every step taken is a step back into history, and I breathed deeply of the atmosphere, even on the frequent days when immersed in a chill mist and drizzle. We lived in a third-floor flat, which we rented for five pounds a week. The only heat was a small gas-fired space heater. By placing a shilling in the heater and standing directly in front of it, we could stay reasonably warm for a two-hour period. Our bedroom was unheated. We were permitted one bath per week, the time pre-established so that our landlady would turn on the manual water heater. Across the street from our flat was a butcher shop that usually adorned its front window with the head of a freshly slaughtered pig, looking outward. We frequently purchased steak mince there and went to the vegetable monger and the fish monger for other daily staples. Milk was delivered by a horse-drawn cart that went from street to street. Mary Kay worked as a medical secretary in the Royal Hospital for Sick Children. Using earphones, she typed dictated manuscripts, desperately trying to understand medical terms delivered in a Scottish accent. The classrooms at the seminary were always cold. I quickly came to value wool clothing; it is much warmer than cotton or artificial fabrics. And I came to understand that the academic robe was not a ceremonial garb worn on festive occasions; it was worn daily by my professors to stay warm. A welcome respite was the mid-morning tea break, when both faculty and students would gather in the great hall for tea and conversation. A cup of tea and a "biscuit" (cookie) cost a "thropny" (three pence), which included tax. (I unhappily paid the tax on tea, even though I had thought that issue had been settled back in Boston!) Education was traditional and classical, with strong emphasis on the theology of Luther and Calvin, patristic doctrines (in Greek!), and biblical studies. By sheer good fortune or by the grace of God, I managed to pass Hebrew by anticipating that the final exam would be to translate the book of Jonah from Hebrew to English. I studied Jonah fanatically in both languages. Had the professor selected any other passage to be translated, I would have failed miserably.

 Returning to the United States, I completed my theological training at Drew Theological School in Madison, New Jersey, graduating in

1968. Again, Mary Kay was the breadwinner, working as a secretary for the Phillips Petroleum Company. I modestly contributed with a summer job, painting dormitory rooms and working as a youth pastor in the Basking Ridge Presbyterian Church. The late '60s were turbulent times. The war in Vietnam had divided the nation. Well-intentioned people endorsed the war; other well-intentioned people, including Mary Kay and me, worked and lobbied to get out of Vietnam, joining in a large protest march with hundreds of thousands in New York City. I volunteered to go door-to-door to help campaign for "Clean Gene" McCarthy, a candidate for the presidency who strongly opposed the war. He never came close to attaining the nomination. April 1968 saw the assassination of Martin Luther King Jr., a tragic event followed by large racial demonstrations, fires, and lootings in numerous American cities. Newark, New Jersey, was especially violent, and some of my seminary colleagues were asked to ride in the police cars to try to calm angry crowds.

"Take thou authority to preach the Word ..." Those words, humbling, challenging, and overwhelming as they are, were pronounced over me during my ordination in June 1968. Of course, no bishop has that authority by virtue of his or her own power. It is an authority that comes from a God who graciously has revealed himself in Hebrew and Christian Scripture and undoubtedly in the sacred writings of other faiths as well. For me, preaching was always the most wonderful and the most terrifying part of my vocation. To preach is to experience a high that is as exciting as any experience this life can offer. But to stand before a congregation and to dare to proclaim not my opinion but the Word of God is intimidating, fearful, and filled with anxiety. In forty some years of preaching, I never slept well the night before. And in my early years, I suffered stomach cramps and diarrhea in the early hours of every Sunday morning, the result of stress and apprehension. I found relief by taking the attitude that I would always preach to myself and hope that others were listening in.

In the United Methodist Church, bishops appoint clergy to local churches. Following ordination (June 11, 1968), I was appointed to be the associate pastor of Hiss United Methodist Church in Baltimore. The church was located on a busy thoroughfare and was broken into on numerous occasions. As we lived in the parsonage next door, we decided to buy an Irish Setter to provide some degree of protection. Mary Kay accepted a position as a medical secretary at Johns Hopkins Hospital. I was privileged to work with a gifted and experienced senior pastor, Charles Niner, from whom I gained many insights into the many skills needed to administer a large church and to pastor a diverse congregation.

There are great events in history that people will remember as long as they live, events that they personally experienced and that left an impact on their lives. Members of my generation can tell you where they were and what they were doing on several unforgettable days: the assassination of President Kennedy (November 22, 1963), the collapse of the Berlin Wall (November 9, 1989), and the attack of 9/11 (September 11, 2001). Among those events was a momentous achievement of scientific technology: the landing of Neil Armstrong and Buzz Aldrin on the moon (July 20, 1969). Mary Kay and I happened to be on vacation, visiting her parents in Billings, Montana. We had taken a day trip to tour the Pryor Mountains, a scenic area near the Wyoming border. Emerging from the darkness of Crater Ice Cave into brilliant sunshine, we heard the news on the car radio that the landing was successful.

The life of a pastor's spouse can be difficult. In June 1970, in the ninth month of her first pregnancy, Mary Kay and I moved to an appointment of my own—three small country churches in Harford County, Maryland, the East Harford Charge. This meant that we were going through the trauma of packing, moving, and unpacking just before the birth of our first child. As we drove to the Greater Baltimore Medical Center on the morning of July 2, it seemed that everything was going normally. But arriving at the hospital, we soon learned that something was dreadfully wrong and that an emergency Caesarean operation would have to be performed immediately. Thanks to the considerable skill of Dr. Artemis Panayis, and by the grace of God, Byron Edward Brought, named after me and his two grandfathers, was born safely.

The people of East Harford were truly "salt of the earth" people—caring, hard-working, and with no pretensions. Our young family was frequently blessed with gifts of homemade rolls and garden vegetables, as well as the labor of men who put new siding on the parsonage. Over the years, worship attendance increased, and small improvements were made—very small improvements. After installing an electric light in the outhouse next to one of the churches, a parishioner remarked, "Now we can see the snakes." I still hold in fond memory the simple faith exhibited by men and women of the parish. I share one example among many. A local funeral director, Howard K. McComas III, was a member of one of the churches. He believed that everyone should receive a dignified funeral, no matter how poor, no matter what their circumstances. Occasionally, the police would deliver the body of an indigent who could not be identified. Howard and I would take the deceased to a burial field owned by the county. There were no flowers, no artificial grass, no tent, no vault, just a field with weeds up to our hips and a hole in the ground. With ropes, we would lower the body into the ground. I read some Scripture and prayed the traditional prayers, and one of God's precious children, unknown to us, was returned to his Creator.

A second son, Andrew Cammack Brought, was born in December 1975, six months before our family moved to Salem United Methodist Church, in the Hebbville community on the west side of Baltimore. The congregation was an Evangelical United Brethren Church before that denomination merged with the Methodist Church in 1968, and many of its families were descendants of the German farmers who had first settled in the area. The building had been erected by faith and sacrifice in the early 1800s, at the huge cost of seventy-five dollars. To raise the money, the congregation gathered for an all-day event of singing, preaching, praying, and passing the plate. Late that night, they had $74.90. Everyone had given all that they had. One old farmer spoke up, "I have ten cents at home; I shall get it and bring it here." His wife immediately objected, "That is our bread money." The old farmer was resolute. "The Lord will provide." Now, this man lived a mile away, and it was dark. Nonetheless, he walked home and returned with the ten cents. The faith that the Lord will provide kept the church alive through my ministry and beyond.

Our lives at Salem were heavily impacted by two events. In the late 1970s Vietnamese "boat people" became refugees in the United States.

Salem Church sponsored one family, providing living quarters, food, and necessities. One of our parishioners, an official at a paper goods factory, provided a job for the father. The family arrived with nearly nothing. Their only possessions were the clothes they were wearing and a Bible that they had preserved in the escape from the Communist takeover. Since it was winter, a kind person in the United Methodist missions office in New York, their port of entry, had given them each a coat. Over time, the family prospered and fully became part of the American way of life. We also welcomed into our home a foster daughter, an eleven-year-old girl named Judy Blouse. She was our next-door neighbor, in the care of her grandmother. With the death of her grandmother, Judy came to live with us for a period of four years. Although her growing-up years had many challenges and difficulties, she successfully matured to womanhood, married, and became a loving and caring mother.

Parents often become close friends with the parents of their children's friends. That certainly became true for us as we moved to Glenmont United Methodist Church in June 1981. Going to our sons' soccer and baseball games became a regular part of life, as is the case for so many American families. We formed relationships with other parents that have remained precious throughout our lives. At Glenmont, I gained some hands-on, self-taught learning. I was now head of a staff and that meant learning how to delegate responsibilities and trusting in the skill of colleagues. Once again, our family expanded. A German high school student, Dominick Trautvetter, came to live with us for a year. His command of English was outstanding, and he easily became another son in our home. Years later, I was privileged to perform his marriage ceremony in Berlin, albeit struggling through a service that undoubtedly sounded more like Pennsylvania Dutch than German. Our appointment at Glenmont ended early and unexpectedly, as I was asked to become the superintendent of the Annapolis district just before Christmas 1985. It is extremely hard to say good-bye to dear friends at the same time you are conducting the Christmas Eve services. And it was hard for our sons to once again pack up, move to new schools, and make new friends. Such is the way of life for itinerant preachers, military families, and many others in a mobile style of life.

The Annapolis district consisted of eighty-four congregations that stretched along the Chesapeake Bay from Glen Burnie to Solomons Island. A diverse area, it included the southern suburbs of Baltimore, the state capital city of Annapolis, and the small communities of farmers and watermen in southern Maryland. Many were undergoing a radical transition in their lives, because traditional tobacco farming and fishing for crabs and oysters were coming to an end. In addition, suburban sprawl was expanding out of both Washington, DC, and Baltimore. Some of the churches were flourishing; others were struggling to survive. It became apparent that congregations that were turned inward, focused on paying the bills, maintaining the facility, or settling internal arguments, would exist in a constant state of near collapse. Congregations that were turned outward, fully involved in reaching out to their communities with loving service and fellowship, would thrive. Yet even in dying churches there are saints of the Lord, whose work and compassion are to be praised. I drove many miles during those years and frequently did not arrive home until the late evening. Fortunately, many church suppers and servings of sweet potato pie kept me going.

Part of life's transitions is watching your children grow up and leave home. With many tears and a choking in our throats, Mary Kay and I delivered older son Byron to Lebanon Valley College and said our farewell. A big part of life had ended. We experienced the same sadness when Andrew left home for Virginia Tech several years later. Now, of course, we know this was right and normal in the passages of life experiences that all must encounter in one way or another. And before long, we discovered it was not so bad after all. Perhaps all of life is like that. Even radical changes bring new opportunities and blessings. And it is extremely helpful to the keep faith of fathers and mothers in the past: "You show me the path of life. In your presence there is fullness of joy; in your right hand are pleasures forevermore" (Psalm 16:11).

The district included a large number of African American Methodists, and I was greatly blessed to serve with and among their pastors and laity. Worship styles were different, but we were one in the Lord, and I always felt at home when I had the experience of being in the minority. It was considered a great honor to become a superintendent, a position with some prestige and a higher salary than most pastors receive. I am truly grateful for the opportunity, and especially to Bishop Joseph Yeakel, for his outstanding leadership and skillful administration of the Book of Discipline. But I remained a pastor at heart and was grateful to return to the pastoral ministry at the end of my six-year term. In July 1992, I became the senior pastor of Calvary United Methodist Church in Annapolis.

Calvary is located on a prime piece of land on College Creek, within an easy walk of the Maryland State House and the United States Naval Academy. The congregation was highly educated, with many serving in federal or state positions or as staff or faculty at the Academy. Early in my ministry, two devoted women of the church died and left in their estates a combined bequest of more than one million dollars. I was extremely impressed that the congregation decided to invest that money and use the dividends and interest for mission and ministry. A few years later, it enabled us to make a major building expansion that cost $2.5 million. After raising one million in a capital funds drive, the church borrowed from the invested bequests for construction, paying itself back at a reasonable rate of 4 percent, less than would have been charged borrowers from a bank and more than a bank would pay depositors in interest.

Though Calvary had a large staff and an extremely able secretary, I had to finally come into the computer age. The old Remington portable typewriter I had used from my college days had both advantages and disadvantages. In all the years I used it, it never once broke down, and I never had to call in a guru to figure out why it was not working. But by then, it was extremely obsolete and limited. Changing ribbons, making corrections with Wite-Out, and being restricted from all the functions a computer could accomplish finally made the decision to use a computer the only intelligent course of action. Even today, the computer is both a curse and a blessing for one who for so many years used a typewriter and a slide rule.

On the morning of September 11, 2001, I was working in my office. Our secretary buzzed me to tell me that a plane had crashed into one of the towers of the World Trade Center. My immediate assumption was that a small plane had crashed, and I wondered how such a thing could have happened on a clear day. Checking the news on my computer, I quickly discovered it was a large passenger jet and that a second plane had also crashed. People meeting in the church that day came spilling out of the classroom, and one of them asked, "What is happening." Without thinking, I responded, "We're at war." The disbelief and shock were overwhelming for everyone. The towers of the World Trade Center were massive—250,000 tons each, with every floor an acre in size. They housed 430 companies with 35,000 employees, and in addition, some 70,000 tourists passed through the buildings daily. We were also immediately concerned about some of our church members and acquaintances who worked at the Pentagon, which also was under attack. Fortunately, they had survived. The church sanctuary is always open for prayer, and occasionally individuals enter for a time of quiet meditation. But on that day, many—both from inside the church and those passing by—entered the sanctuary for prayer.

It was at Calvary that I lived through and experienced my biggest professional disappointment. For several years, there was a strong push to bring casinos into the state. Strong arguments were made that huge proceeds would benefit the schoolchildren, and that since Delaware and West Virginia already had casinos, Maryland should have them also. I strongly objected on moral and economic grounds too numerous to adequately explain in this diversion. Although I testified many times before the Maryland House of Delegates, my efforts were inadequate to keep casinos out of the state. To this day, I confess that failure before God and apologize to fellow citizens for my inabilities. I did learn an especially painful lesson. For several years, we were successful, and the House of Delegates defeated proposed slot legislation. At that time a Republican governor was trying to bring in slots. Republican delegates supported slots; Democrats opposed them. Since Democrats in the House held the majority, the bills were defeated. I naively assumed that the delegates supporting my position were acting in a moral and noble manner. It was not so. A Democrat was elected governor who pushed for slots. And there was a sea change in the House: the Republicans who had supported slots now opposed them, and Democrats who had opposed slots now supported the legislation. Again holding the majority, Democrats won the battle, and casinos are here—and are still growing in number. It is not only individuals that become addicted to gambling; state governments become addicted as well.

Surely there must be a better way for government to function.

##  The Lie

There is a lie that leads to death, and there is a truth that leads to life. There is a lie that plunges us into darkness, and there is a truth that allows the light to come streaming in. There is a lie that, as long as we live in its delusion, will hold us captive in a sick and sordid state. And there is a truth that can transform us.

What is this lie? And what is this truth?

"If we say we have no sin, we deceive ourselves, and the truth is not in us. If we confess our sins, he who is faithful and just will forgive our sins and cleanse us from all unrighteousness" (1 John 1:8–9).

It is easy to live in a deception, to ignore the sin that is in our lives. We think that all is well, that we are moving forward and progressing nicely, and that we are saving ourselves through our hard work, our technological advances, our affluent lifestyle, and our material success. We pretend that sin and death have no stranglehold over us. But it is all a lie. It will all end in the grave. That is nothing that death will not take away from us. We are all on a death march. Our condition is terminal.

Of course, we realize that not all is well, but that becomes the occasion to blame someone else and find a scapegoat for life's problems. It legitimates our anger, wraps us up in a comfortable blanket of self-pity, and avoids any suggestion of responsibility. Why is my marriage on the rocks? It is because my partner has failed to live up to my expectations. Why am I failing in my business? It is because the system is tilted against me. Why am I doing so poorly in school? It is because my teacher is no good. Why am I alienated from my faith? It is because twenty years ago, a religious leader said something that upset me. Not only individuals but whole societies have great expertise in passing blame. Why is the economy struggling? Obviously, it is the policies of the liberals (if you are a conservative) and the policies of the conservatives (if you are a liberal).

To live in the lie is fatal, because it prevents me from making the changes I need to make.

I need to face the truth, and that truth is that I need to be forgiven, and I need the grace of God. It is not just the terrorist who needs to be forgiven, not just the cult leader who needs to be forgiven, not just the drug dealer who needs to be forgiven, and it is not just the jerk who lives next door, or the angry spouse, or the rebellious teenager who needs to be forgiven. I need to be forgiven.

If a ship is headed toward an iceberg, the captain needs to change course. It will do no good to ignore the iceberg. It will do no good to keep the same direction. And so in our lives, we need to repent (to use the biblical word for a change in course). We need to turn around, turn away from self, and turn into a positive and honest relationship with God and with others. And when we do, pardon and grace abounds. There is the possibility of new life.

In the gospel stories, sinners and tax collectors eat and drink with Jesus; religious elders and Pharisees condemn him to death. The sinners and tax collectors understood that they were lost and that their only hope was the gracious pardon of God. Religious leaders thought that they did not need to be forgiven and that they did not need saving grace. In living that lie, they remained in the darkness.

Let there be no mistake: there is a lie that leads to death, and there is a truth that leads to life. If we accept the truth, the truth will set us free. Then the lost will be found. And once found, they will be lost no more.

# The Hard One

Love your enemies (Matthew 5:43). This commandment of Jesus is outrageously difficult. But like a private in the army, I am under command. I must do it. And it does make some sense. If ever there is to be peace in the world, if ever the cycle of continuing conflict is to be broken, if ever there is to be any hope of reconciliation, I must love my enemy. I do not want to do it. But it must be done. I must pray for the softening of hardened hearts. I must forgive. I must work for a brighter future. I must be willing to reach out in kindness.

To love my enemy is difficult.

But there is a commandment that is even more difficult than that.

Love your neighbor (Matthew 22:39). To love my neighbor is to love the irritable jerk who lives down the street, the gossip-filled woman who goes to my church, the vandalizing teenager who spray-painted my fence, the friend who betrayed and broke confidence, the family member whose bitter words cut deeply into my heart, and all those petty nitpickers who launch painful insults and criticisms on a regular basis. These are not a faceless enemy from a foreign land but the people I see every day. And I am under command to somehow love each one of them.

Love your neighbor.

That is the hard one.

## The Fire Alarm

"Whoever comes to me and does not hate father and mother, wife and children, brothers and sisters, yes, and even life itself, cannot be my disciple. Whoever does not carry the cross and follow me cannot be my disciple. … None of you can become my disciple if you do not give up all your possessions" (Luke 14:26–27, 33).

Karl Marx once said that religion is the opiate of the people. It is obvious that Karl Marx had not read these words of Jesus when he made that statement. This is not an opiate. These demands are ludicrous.

No preacher would ever invite someone to become a member of his/her congregation by using this text. In forty years of ministry, I frequently said, "Come to our church. You will make many new friends here. We have a wonderful choir and outstanding educational opportunities. There is a delightful coffee and fellowship time after each service." I never once said, "If you come, you must give up everything you have, renounce even your own life, and struggle along with a cross on your back. And by the way, if you don't hate your wife, children, and parents, don't even think about coming." Good preachers don't say that. They know how to play the crowd.

Likewise, politicians know how to get support. Tell people what they want to hear. Manipulate the masses. If it is a conservative crowd, talk about tax cuts and family values, and be sure to tell them that everyone gets to keep their semiautomatic, no matter how deranged or unstable one might be. If it is a liberal crowd, talk about global warming and medical benefits, and be sure to mention that every child should be provided with condoms the moment he or she reaches puberty. Measure your words carefully, offend no one, let them all think that you have their interests at heart.

To make Jesus' words even more outrageous, consider the context. "Large crowds were traveling with him" (Luke 14:25). Jesus was finally getting somewhere. People were beginning to take notice. Huge crowds were listening to every word. What an opportunity! What could the modern preacher or politician do in this setting! Yet Jesus speaks words that seem intentionally designed to drive everyone away. What does he think he is doing?

When the glass is shattered and a fire alarm sounds, the resulting noise is loud, harsh, and obnoxious. It is not a soft and pleasant sound that gently lulls you to sleep. It is intentionally designed to arouse you to action. You cannot sit there indifferently. You must do something about it.

Jesus' strong words are clearly not to be interpreted literally. A literal interpretation, like a literal interpretation of the opening chapters of Genesis, makes a laughingstock out of the gospel. By using strong language, the Lord intentionally says what we preachers are afraid to say: there is a cost to discipleship. Being a follower of Jesus is not an easy task. It will (not might, but will) involve radical trust, sacrifice, and the transformation of one's life. It will require loving people whom you cannot stand, forgiving people who have hurt you deeply, and putting the needs of others before your own needs. It will require that you persistently pray for and work for a world where the downtrodden receive justice, where all God's children have this day their daily bread, and where conflict gives way to peace. To dare to follow Jesus will be the defining decision of your life.

The fire alarm is sounding. It must not be ignored.

## The Proposal

There are invitations, and there are invitations. Some invitations are open-ended and indefinite; a reply is neither expected nor needed. "Y'all come over and see us sometime." You do not have to respond to that kind of invitation. You are welcome to drop by for a visit, if you feel like it, but if you never get around to it, it is quite all right. It is simply a loose and general invitation that really doesn't matter if you accept it or not.

But there is a second kind of invitation, one that presents a specific and direct request, and for that kind of invitation, a definite response is required. "Sweetheart, will you marry me?" The proposal to marriage is all-encompassing and life-changing. Whether you answer yes or no, it will be a defining moment that will have an enormous influence on the rest of your life. But you must answer. You cannot let that invitation go unanswered. You must choose, and you must act upon your decision.

When Jesus extends an invitation, what kind of invitation does he offer? "Peter and Andrew, follow me and I will make you fishers of men" (Matthew 4:19). "Matthew, leave your tax booth and follow me" (Matthew 9:9). "Thomas, do you believe, now that you have seen?" (John 20:29). "Simon, son of John, do you love me?" (John 21:15).

Do these sound like vague and loose questions, casually mentioned? Or are they very specific, very personal, and very much calling for an answer? Is Jesus saying, "Y'all come and see me sometime?" Or is he saying "I want you to be mine. I want you to be my lover, my friend, my companion, and my partner. I want you to embrace me and to embrace my way of life. I want you to love as I love, to forgive as I forgive, to serve as I serve. I want you to live with me forever."

There is nothing more irresponsible than to assume that it really does not matter whether I answer the call of Jesus or not, that it does not matter whether I am committed or not, that it does not affect my life or the life of anyone else, one way or another, and that the answer can be put off until another time. The gracious invitation of Jesus does not mean, "I love you; therefore, you can rest, secure in your wanton self-centeredness and remain in the arms of your own agenda." It means, "I love you; I call you to a new life, a transformed life of grace and peace. I urge you to be mine. But be assured, I will tolerate no other lovers."

The invitation has been offered. A proposal has been made. And each of us must answer.

## Free to Go

His close friend and colleague, James, the brother of John, had met a grisly end, beheaded by a long and heavy sword. Now it was his turn. In fearful silence, he waited for the executioner to come. Two sets of chains were tightly squeezed upon his ankles and wrists. On either side, two soldiers stood constant watch, even when he was sleeping. Sentries guarded his prison door day and night. There was no chance he could escape. But under the sovereign grace of God, there was no chance that he would *not* escape. A light shone in his dank, dark cell. His chains fell off, with a heavy clank ringing from the stone floor. As he walked out the door, passing the guards and sentries, the large iron gate that led to the city opened of its own accord. He was set free—free to live another day, free to embrace his family and friends, free to go about his work and ministry. Peter was free to go (Acts 12:1–11).

This story is not a fairy tale. It is real. It really happened, just the way that Luke tells it. It was a miracle, to be sure, but it is not the real miracle. The real miracle is that it happens again and again and again.

Peter's story is our story. What happened to Peter is offered to us. We are free to go.

No, we are not set free from a literal prison with literal chains and literal shackles. We are set free from an even stronger captor. We are set free from the reign of sin, and we are set free from the dominion of death. There is no earthly chance we can escape them. But in Jesus Christ, sin is forgiven and death is overcome. Sin and death no longer have power over our lives. We are free to go.

We are free to go from bitterness and hatred and the vengeful desire to get even with someone who has harmed us. We are free to go from prejudice and bigotry toward those who are different, for all people, however different, are God's children. We are free to go from the daily worry of what we are going to eat, or what we are going to drink, or what we are going to wear, for when we seek God's kingdom first, all these things will be ours as well (Matthew 6:31–33). We are free to go from fear and anxiety, for there is nothing that can destroy the ultimate fulfillment that God has purposed for us. We are free to go about our lives, free to love, free to serve, free to forgive, free to give thanks, free to rejoice, and free to finally be at peace. We are free.

What a marvelous thing it would be if suddenly you were set free from credit card, car loan, and mortgage debt. You would celebrate a wondrous freedom, released from the encumbrances of debt. Your joy would be unspeakable.

There is an even greater freedom, an even greater joy. It is the glorious freedom of the children of God. And it is freely offered to all.

The light shines. The chains are falling off. There is a creaking sound as the iron gate opens.

Arise and go forth!

You are free to go.

# ❂ The Well

When the Bible speaks of a wilderness, it is not referring to a land of trees and forests, of running deer and wandering bears, of swiftly flowing mountain streams that form deep pools around large round stones, or of ferns and laurel and may apples that brighten the leaf-covered ground. In biblical lands, wilderness is an inhospitable place—dry and barren, a place of coarse and rocky ravines and stretching sands, lifeless save for insects and reptiles that somehow have adapted to survive the scorching heat.

Such was the wilderness of Beersheba, some seventeen centuries before the birth of Christ. For Hagar, it was a place of death. For some time now, she had lived a reasonably comfortable life as a servant to Sarah and as a companion to Abraham. At the suggestion of Sarah, she had borne a son, Ishmael, for Abraham. But then Sarah herself became pregnant and bore a son for Abraham, Isaac. Unable to tolerate the presence of another woman and another son competing for the love, devotion, and attention of Abraham, Sarah drove her servant and Ishmael out of the family tent and into the wilderness.

Abandoned and frightened, Hagar faced the dangers and perils of a hostile wilderness. When the last of the water in the skin ran out, Hagar knew she was doomed. She could not bear the thought of watching little Ishmael perish, so she placed him under a small bush and then went off "about the distance of a bowshot" and, weeping pitifully, waited to die. It was then that a remarkable thing took place; indeed, what might be considered a miracle of grace. "God opened her eyes and she saw a well of water. She went, and filled the skin with water, and gave the boy a drink" (Genesis 21:8–21).

A compassionate God had spared the life of Hagar and Ishmael, the son who, like Isaac, would become the father of a great nation (Genesis 21:18). In mercy, God heard Hagar's cry, and God acted. The God of the Bible is more than the limitless power that brought the universe into being, more than the infinite, more than the beyond. God is personal.

God cares. God hears the cry of a desperate and dying woman in a wilderness. And in saving grace, God takes action.

Notice how God chose to act. The Scripture does not say that God spoke a word of command, as God chose to do at the beginning of creation, to suddenly and miraculously bring a well of water into existence. God opened her eyes. The well was already there. The source of life was already present and readily available. Hagar just needed to have her eyes opened to see the grace that was already there. That was the miracle that God performed.

Let us not be blind to your miracles, O God. Open our eyes to see the possibilities of peace in a world of conflict, the moments of grace in the midst of doubt, and the dawning of light in a darkened sky. And in the most desolate and parched wilderness that we might ever encounter, open our eyes to the well.

## The Four-Letter Word

There is a four-letter word that is ugly and demeaning, a word so obscene that it must be avoided by people of every race and culture. It is a word that turns us inward, a word that, in small and nearly imperceptible ways, leads to division and separation, conflict, and war. It is a word that unleashes harmful thoughts and destructive acts. Worst of all, it is a word that undermines the glorious nobility and majesty purposed for every person by the Creator of us all.

Mine.

## Controlled

I am very comfortable with the way that the New Revised Standard Version of the Bible translates 2 Corinthians 5:14: "the love of Christ urges us on." I like that. It is a nice and pleasant little thought—Christ's love urges us on. It encourages us, it affirms us, and it gives us helpful support. This is a very comfortable verse indeed.

But I am not so comfortable with other translations. "The love of Christ controls us" states the Revised Standard Version. Good News for Modern Man says, "We are ruled by the love of Christ." Christ's love controls us, rules us, directs us, and governs our behavior and our attitudes. The old King James Version goes so far as to put it this way: "The love of Christ constraineth us."

I don't want to be controlled. I don't want to be ruled. And who in their right minds would ever want to be constrained? It is certainly much easier to be urged on.

But maybe I need to be controlled. Maybe some constraint would be helpful. I need to control my greed. I need to control my pride. I need to control my lust. And I surely need to control my tongue, my prejudices, my sarcasm, and my selfishness.

To be controlled by the love of Christ means that I am not controlled by my own agenda. It means that I am not controlled by the standards of the world. I am not controlled by the past or by anything that has happened in the past. I am not controlled by a drive to get even with someone who harmed me. I am not controlled by questionable ambitions. I am not content to do something because everyone else is doing it.

I need to be constrained. I need to be controlled by something higher than myself. I need the love of Christ to be the ruling principle in my life.

And maybe you need it too.

The next time you hear malicious gossip about a neighbor, refrain from joining in. Instead, share something that you appreciate about that neighbor. The next time your husband or wife is terribly upset, don't push the hot button that will drive him or her over the edge. Instead, speak the soft answer that turns away wrath (Proverbs 15:1). The next time some idiot cuts you off on the highway, don't respond with an angry gesture. Instead, realize that at that moment, the most important thing you have to do is to get yourself and your passengers safely to your destination.

It is not easy to be a follower of Christ. It was never intended to be. But it is incredibly liberating.

I am no longer controlled by the world or its ways. I am a new creation (2 Corinthians 5:17). I am controlled by the love of Christ.

## ✦ Unwilling Servants

What we want to do and what we should do may be as far removed as the ice-covered land mass of Antarctica is from the burning sands of the Sahara Desert.

I may not want to serve on a church committee, teach a Sunday school class, or help with the Vacation Bible School. I may have no desire to serve a meal in a homeless shelter, go on a mission project to a place I never heard of, or install drywall in a home being erected by Habitat for Humanity. I may despise having to relate to some annoying and aggravating people, whom I would avoid if I possibly could do so. But what I want to do and what I should do are two entirely different things. If my arm is twisted, or if I am begged and cajoled, or if my conscience nags me enough, I may find myself doing what I do not want to do. Ironically, like the friend of Sam-I-Am eating green eggs and ham, I may discover that I actually enjoy the experience and benefit from it.

There are patron saints of all those who must do what they do not want to do. There are patron saints for all of us.

Gregorius Anicius was born in AD 540, the son of a privileged and deeply religious family. The mid-sixth century was a troubled time. Rome had been sacked, and a great civilization was replaced by a long period considered to be the Dark Ages in Europe, when culture, science, and art would nearly disappear. Plague swept throughout Italy, and one-third of its population—sometimes entire families—succumbed to the disease. Gregorius grew up to become a monk and thoroughly loved his calling. He devoted himself to revitalizing worship, promoting the use of liturgical plainsong that now honors his name, the Gregorian chant.

Against all his desires and wishes, Gregorius became Pope Gregory I. He bemoaned the demanding responsibilities of office and all the secular burdens that the papacy entailed. He simply wanted to live a monastic life, in quiet and peaceful contemplation, withdrawn from the dealings of this fallen world. Unwillingly, he served, and he instituted a title of papacy still used by popes today: *servus servorum Dei*—servant of the servants of God.

There was an experience in the life of Pope Gregory I that left a lasting impression upon him. He had seen English slaves sold in a Roman market and was grieved by way in which fellow human beings—sons and daughters of God—were being treated. He believed they should be treated with love, respect, and decency and that they should be taught the good news of Christian faith. And so, in AD 595, he commissioned a fellow monk named Augustine to lead a mission of forty monks to England, to bring Christianity to the Anglo-Saxon pagans who lived in that faraway land. (This was not Augustine of Hippo, the great theologian who wrote *Civitas Dei*, or *The City of God*, but a Benedictine monk who lived some two centuries later.)

Augustine and his colleagues started out on their journey, but it was not long before they abandoned their mission. And who could blame them? Who would desire to leave the Mediterranean climate and venture to a remote land of chill and drizzle? Who would want to depart from friends and family amid the high probability that they would never see them again? Who would be eager to face the overwhelming task of bringing Christian faith to those embracing pagan customs? And so Augustine went back to Rome.

Now, in church history, Pope Gregory I is often called "Gregory the Great." That is not by accident. Gregory was a strong and dominant personality and an uncompromising evangelist. Some of his methods were questionable. He converted Jews in Italy by bribing them, and in Sardinia, he had nonbelievers flogged and imprisoned. (That is one way to increase church attendance!) Gregory was not a man who would take no for an answer. He insisted that Augustine go to England; there was no other option.

So Augustine and his colleagues went forth again, landing in Kent, on the shores of southeastern England, in the spring of 597. They encountered a woman named Bertha, who was not a typical Anglo Saxon woman of her day. She was a Christian woman of royal birth, who had come to England from France to be the wife of Aethelbert, the king of Kent. Between the efforts of Augustine and Bertha, Aethelbert became a Christian, and with his conversion, thousands of his subjects became Christian as well. Augustine continued his mission, turning pagan places of worship into Christian churches. One of the reconsecrated sites is now the location of Canterbury Cathedral.

A pope who did not want to be pope and a missionary who did not want to go brought Christianity to England.

Perhaps the overriding issue is not what we want to do but what needs to be done. Not our will, but God's.

Lord, give me the grace to go where I may not want to go, to do what I may not want to do, to serve in ways I may not want to serve, and to love the people I may not want to love.

##  The Table

It is a long table, extremely long, and yes, wide as well, stretching outward as far as the eye can see and even beyond. The guests are seated, and quite a mixed and motley group they are. They have come from every land and language, every race and color. A few are known and recognized, but most have not yet been introduced. On the table are bread and wine, small servings to be sure but quite sufficient. Just one crumb, just one drop is more than enough. And after all, this is only the appetizer, the foretaste of a greater banquet yet to come. It is the table of the Lord.

We do not get to choose who is seated at the table.

We do not get to choose our brothers and sisters. When we are born, if we are privileged to be born into a family, we have no say in whether we have brothers or sisters, or how many, or who they happen to be. If my sister could have chosen a brother when we were growing up, she surely would not have chosen me.

When married couples get divorced and then marry other partners, their children often find themselves seated at the dinner table with brothers and sisters they did not have before. They may have been only children, and they may not have known these other youth and children, but suddenly, they have new brothers and sisters in the family. They were not given a choice.

When my sons were young, my wife and I received a foster daughter into our home. She lived with us for four years. Our sons were accustomed to ruling the roost, but suddenly, they had to contend with a sister—a sister whom they did not choose. They had to learn to live together, to share toys, and to accept the reality that sometimes Mom's or Dad's attention would be directed to someone else. It was not an easy adjustment, but they made it, because that's just the way it was.

And so it is with that table that is the Lord's, stretching outward to vast and incomprehensible distances, surrounded by countless guests. For if the Lord is Lord of only part of the earth or the Lord of only other generations, he is not Lord. The Lord is Lord of all the earth, of all times and places, of all peoples and nations, and of all that is or ever will be. "God shows no partiality, but in every nation anyone who fears Him and does what is right is acceptable to Him" (Acts 10:34–35).

Some seated at the table of the Lord are dear friends and family members. What a joy to eat and drink with them! Some who gather at the table are complete strangers with unfamiliar faces. And there are some at the table with whom we have had arguments, hard feelings, disputes, and conflicts. We might be quite surprised to see them there. But they are there, and like it or not, they are now our brothers and sisters. If we are to sit at the Lord's table, we must welcome them as such.

Come to the table, for the meal is ready. And bid warm welcome to the brothers and sisters who are dining with you.

## Holy Communion

It is not so much something that we do as something that we receive.

It is only a small piece of bread, a small sip of wine. Yet it is an extraordinary gift of God. It is the visible, tangible, taste-able reminder that Christ died for us. It is the means by which God imparts his covenant of forgiveness and saving grace (Matthew 26:28). It is a foretaste of a banquet when "many will come from east and west and will eat with Abraham and Isaac and Jacob in the kingdom of heaven" (Matthew 8:11).

No one is so sinful that he or she should stay away. No one is so righteous that he or she should stay away.

We come to the Lord's Table not because of what we are but in spite of what we are; not because we are good and pure and noble, but because we are selfish, greedy, and irritable; not because we are worthy, but because we stand in the grip of sin and death.

Ragged clothes and haggard faces cannot keep us from his love and neither can our petty, narrow, bitter spirits. If we come to his table with open hearts, we shall receive mercy. If we open our minds to grace, we shall receive the new life that he freely offers to all. "If we confess our sins, he who is faithful and just will forgive our sins and cleanse us from all unrighteousness" (1 John 1:9).

Christ died for us. *He* died for us. His body was broken and his blood drained out that we might live. He loved us that much. And that makes all the difference.

Eat the bread. Drink the wine. "O taste and see that the Lord is good" (Psalm 34:8a).

# The Stained-Glass Window

I stood in awe before the stained-glass window. Like many stained-glass windows, it told a story. Pictured was Jesus, standing in a pastoral scene of green grassland and gently flowing water. The Lord was holding a lamb in his arms. It was an artistic portrayal of Christ's words, "I am the good shepherd" (John 10:11).

But it was not the picture that caught my attention, though I readily affirm that "the Lord is my shepherd" (Psalm 23:1). It was the color red. Jesus was wearing a red robe, and the red was as beautiful a color as I have ever seen. A deep, vivid red, rich and magnificent in hue, it was that redness that was alive in sheer loveliness.

Now, I say that the glass in Jesus' robe was red. Technically and scientifically, the sunlight coming through the glass is composed of many wavelengths, some of which make up the visible spectrum. The particular piece of red glass absorbed all the colors of the spectrum except for red. The red wavelengths passed through the glass, to be seen by the human eye. Which is to say, we call the glass red not because of what it possesses but because of what it allows to shine through.

Our lives are like that too. People will know us not by what we possess but by what we allow to shine through; by what we say and how we say it; what we give and the spirit in which we give it; and what we do and how we do it. We are what we pass on to others.

And if I should go outside the church and look at that stained-glass window, it would be diminished. The red would not be so beautiful. It would be subdued and unimpressive, lost amid indistinct and darkened colors. Indeed, even the shepherd would be lost in an indistinguishable dullness.

The beauty and the message of the stained-glass window can be seen only from the inside, when light from above comes shining through.

# The Diamond

One might easily have passed over it, the mud-encrusted chunk of kimberlite, though even in this condition, it was the marvelous result of an eruption from deep within the earth, many eons ago. But dirty and ordinary, with no particular beauty or value, it was just another piece of dark-colored rock, save for the reflection of what seemed to be a small fragment of dull and embedded glass.

There was one who did not pass over it. Picking it up, this observer carefully studied it and claimed it from the broken pile of ore. It was washed and cleaned, cleaved and marked, and cut with laser beams.

Then, in the hands of a skilled craftsman, that glasslike fragment was precisely polished into fifty-seven facets. No longer dark and stone-like, it now sparkled with the brilliance of reflected light, dazzling white, yet with refractions of myriad colors. Carefully mounted in a jeweler's special creation, it became a precious treasure.

I look upon my own life, and I look upon the lives of others. If I am looking for imperfections, they will readily be found—greed and lust and pride, lurking deep inside the inner souls of all of us. But might there also be a priceless gem that lies within the heart of every child of God, yet to be revealed?

May I have the grace to see the pure and noble, however encrusted by surrounding mud.

# Expectations

With great expectations, I entered the door of the church. I came with the hope that I would hear a challenging and interesting sermon, one that would answer the very concerns and worries that had recently plagued my mind. I came anticipating that the music would be pleasant and uplifting and, of course, the style of music that I enjoy most. I came expecting that the warm fellowship of a caring congregation would be readily seen in welcoming handshakes and friendly smiles. Yes, I had many expectations, but why not? I was coming to a church, and if this church was worth its salt, it should surely satisfy my needs. And if not—if I should leave disappointed, if I should feel that the service was dull and boring, if no one spoke to me, if staying awake was the only challenge the sermon had to offer, if the music was quite mediocre—why should I bother to return? Why should I have faith if religion is weak and ineffectual?

How many people feel that way? As one who has been a pastor for more than forty years, I have undoubtedly made many feel that their expectations were unmet.

But what are my expectations? Preaching? Music? Fellowship? All well and good, definitely a nice part of any church experience. But do I come with a desperate awareness: I need you, Lord. I need to be forgiven. I need to be healed. I need to be changed. I need to have the lust, pride, greed, and resentment removed from my life—the dark shadows that lurk deep within my being. Without you, Lord, I am sick and dying. Without you, I am lost in eternal death.

Do I enter a church expecting to encounter the living God? Do I expect to stand face-to-face with the Alpha and Omega of all things, the almighty Creator of heaven and earth, of the sea and the dry land? Do I expect to experience the presence of the living Christ in such an unmistakable way that I will be shaken out my lethargy and moved beyond my self-centeredness? Do I expect to sense a power of resurrected life so intensely and so personally that sin and death will lose their dominion over me? Do I expect to be transformed into a new creation of love, justice, and mercy (2 Corinthians 5:17)?

Customary Christianity will not save me. Being baptized or married in a church will not save me. Attending worship will not save me. Making a token gift will not save me. Mouthing the words of a creed will not save me. I must come to Jesus like the disciples on a stormy sea: "Save us, Lord, or we shall perish!" (Matthew 8:25). I must come like the father of a child who is critically ill: "I believe, help thou my unbelief" (Mark 9:24).

What are my expectations when I come through the door of a church?

If I come with the wrong expectations, then even if my expectations are fulfilled, I am cheating myself and missing out on a far greater gift.

## ✹ Two Churches or One?

As I look back over the history of Christianity, I believe it is possible to discern the existence of two churches—two churches that exist side by side with each other across the centuries. Two churches that are very different in their motives, their beliefs, and their actions. I am not speaking of the Catholic and Protestant churches, for that difference has only been around for one-fourth of Christian history. And I am not speaking of any denominations, whose differences are quite trivial when compared with all that is held in common. No, the churches of which I speak are not so clearly defined. These two churches are more closely interconnected and strangely intertwined. These two churches have competed with one another for the support and loyalty of followers, and even now, these two churches lay claim to our allegiance.

What are these two churches?

The first church is giving, and caring, and serving. The first church, like its Savior, is willing to lay down its life for the world. It is the church of Peter and Paul and John, of Patrick and Benedict and Francis of Assisi, of Luther and Calvin, of John and Charles and Susannah Wesley, of Albert Schweitzer and Mother Teresa and Martin Luther King. The first church sits up all night with a dying patient, stands in solidarity with the poor and outcast, binds up the wounds of the broken and hurting, and speaks a word of encouragement to the hopeless and despairing. This first church has sacrificed to build hospitals and schools and homes for children and the elderly. It has sent its missionaries into all the world and has translated the Bible into virtually every language known to humankind. This first church is a pioneer in social justice, in education, in health, in literacy, and in peace and reconciliation, and it has the courage to say it is an outrage than any of God's precious children should go this day without their daily bread. This first church has as its motto one simple word: yes. Yes to life. Yes to forgiveness. Yes to new possibilities. Yes to the infinite worth and dignity of every person on the face of this planet. Yes to grace. Yes to the power of God. Yes, yes, yes!

But sadly, we must confess that side by side with this church there exists a second church, a church whose deeds and activities are not so noble. This second church is greedy and manipulative and self-serving and has no purpose but its own. This second church is the church of the scribes and Pharisees (and please do not assume that the Pharisees are a religious institution of two thousand years ago – the Pharisees are children of the twenty-first century: they live on our street, they attend our churches, and they dwell deep down inside our lives). The second church is the church of Ananias and Sapphira, of the narrow-minded men who masterminded the Inquisition, put Galileo on trial, and burned the witches of Salem. It is the church that denies and tries to cover up the abuse of children by its priests, and it is the church that condemns fellow members of the body of Christ whom it judges to be guilty of a self-created sin of "popery." This second church exists to keep its machinery oiled, its coffers filled, and its authority figures in office. It gives its blessing to the status quo and practices the worldly art of getting along with the powers that be, even if those powers are those of Hitler's Germany, Peter Botha's South Africa, or Southern states importing slaves for their plantations. This second church has as its motto one simple word: no. No to plucking grains of wheat on the Sabbath day. No to playing cards. No to going to movies on Sunday. No to married priests. No to women in ministry. No to contemporary music in worship. No to teaching evolution. No, no, no! This second church has lost all sense of integrity and all sense of righteousness; indeed, it has lost all sense whatsoever.

Two churches, side by side over the centuries, competing for our allegiance.

I think that one of our problems, as Christians, is that we settle for so little, when what God intends for us is so great. We are satisfied with mediocrity, when what God intends for us is glory. We are satisfied with being weak and ineffectual, when what God intends is that we should receive a power that can transform the world. We are satisfied with ministering to ourselves, when what God intends is that we should make disciples of all nations (Matthew 28:19). We are, in the analogy of C. S. Lewis, like the little boy who is content to make mud pies in the slums when he could have had a holiday at the sea, because he cannot imagine what a holiday at the sea would be like (C. S. Lewis, *The Weight of Glory and Other Addresses*).

I had a dear and respected aunt, Aunt Laura. When she died, we found scribbled in the margin of her Bible this prayer: "Lord, make me an extraordinary Christian." She was an extraordinary Christian. We settle for being ordinary, like everyone else, when what God intends is that we be extraordinary, following a higher standard than this passing world can ever know. Lord, make me an extraordinary Christian.

What is God's great intention, God's great dream for his people? God gives us gifts "for building up the body of Christ, until all of us come to the unity of the faith and of the knowledge of the Son of God, to maturity, to the measure of the full stature of Christ" (Ephesians 4:12–13).

"The measure of the full stature of Christ"—that is what God wants for each of us and for his church, to be like Christ in all that we think and do and say—in our motives, in our attitudes, in our lifestyle. That is what the Wesleys were talking about when they challenged us to go to perfection. You may not want to go on to perfection. But what, then, are you going on to? God wants us to be like Christ, to reach his full stature, and if we settle for anything less than that, we are cheating ourselves.

To attain "the measure of the full stature of Christ," let God's great dream and intention become our great dream and intention, so that we can become one church—one church that does the will of God. One church that never turns its back on a hungry child or walks away from injustice. One church that demonstrates forgiveness and love. One church that brings healing, reconciliation, and peace. One church that loves the Lord with all its heart and soul and mind (Matthew 22:37). One church that, like John the Baptist, points its finger to the Savior and simply says, "Here is the Lamb of God who takes away the sin of the world!" (John 1:29). One church that knows the glorious liberty of the sons and daughters of God (Romans 8:21). One church that shall never be divided.

By the grace of God we can become that one church.

And what a church that will be!*

# God in Three Persons

Many years ago, I had the privilege of seeing the play *A Man for All Seasons* by Robert Bolt. It is the story of Thomas More, a deeply religious man who was supreme chancellor of England under Henry VIII.

---

\* Note: This offering was previously published in a journal of the Methodist Church in Ireland, the *Methodist Newsletter*, Volume 40, Number 436, November 2012.

While More struggled to be loyal to both God and king, ultimately, his personal convictions would not permit him to sanction Henry's divorce of Catherine of Aragon, nor to acknowledge that Henry was supreme head of the church. Convicted of treason, More was beheaded after speaking the famous last words, "I die the king's good servant but God's first."

As I watched the play, I observed a striking difference between two of the characters. Cardinal Wolsey, who appeared in the early parts of the play, was portrayed as an old man, with a full beard, overweight and pompous, and attired in the most grandiose of ecclesiastical gowns. Although he was a devoted Roman Catholic, Wolsey was quite content to compromise his beliefs in order to carry out Henry's wishes. At the end of the play, another character appeared, Thomas Cranmer. Cranmer was young and clean-shaven, wearing modest clothing. A firmly devoted Protestant, he was strict and stern in his character.

And here is the amazing thing. In the play, I saw that both Wolsey and Cranmer were portrayed by the same actor. With a quick change of costume and makeup, and with considerable skill, one man was able to convincingly portray two very different roles. The old Latin word for these roles, or characters, is *personae*. The English word "person" is derived from this Latin word. When you see a play, you are usually handed a booklet that contains the cast list, the *Dramatis Personae*—the dramatic characters.

Perhaps this illustration will help to understand one of the fundamental doctrines of Christianity, the doctrine of the Trinity. For Christians, the Trinity is the standard definition of God: one God in three persons—Father, Son, and Holy Spirit. Jesus himself commands us to "Go therefore and make disciples of all nations, baptizing them in the name of the Father and of the Son and of the Holy Spirit, and teaching them to obey everything that I have commanded you" (Matthew 28:19–20a). The defining creedal statements of Christian faith, both the Apostles' Creed and the Nicene Creed, contain three paragraphs—one describing the Father, one the Son, and one the Holy Spirit. And some Christians believe that the Trinity is referenced in the first chapter of Genesis, when almighty God, Father, creates all things through the

Word, as the *ruach* of God—wind or Spirit—is moving across the waters of the formless void.

Admittedly, the Trinity is not easy to understand. We think of the word "persons" as referring to distinct, independent, separate, autonomous individuals. How can one be three at the same time? What is meant by Trinity? The faithful of many ages have been puzzled by it, and critics across the centuries have charged that although Christians may claim to be monotheists, they are actually polytheists, worshipping three gods. While Patrick successfully used a shamrock to explain the Trinity to the Irish in the mid-400s, attempts to explain the doctrine have often been ridiculed by nonbelievers.

Perhaps the confusion may be overcome when we go back to the root word, *personae*. We would know nothing of God if God had not revealed himself to us, for God is infinitely beyond the human. Apart from God's self-disclosure, for me to speak of God would be like an ant crawling on the sidewalk, trying to explain to the colony what I might be thinking or doing, or where I might be going, as I walked along. Indeed, the comparison fails, for there is a finite difference between the ant and me, while there is an infinite difference between God and me.

But thanks be to God, God is a God of revelation. God reveals himself and shows us who he is in ways that we can understand. God reveals himself in three *personae*. God is Father, Creator of heaven and earth, the sea and the dry land, infinite in goodness, power, and love, the beginning and the end of all things. God is Son, incarnate in Jesus the Christ, who is Savior, Redeemer, and Lord. And God is Holy Spirit, the spiritual presence of the divine in our midst, in our world, in our lives.

If you wanted to sail to England, you could board a boat and set off on your own. You might get to England that way, or you might end up who knows where. You would be far more likely to arrive in England if you used the tools of navigation that have been successfully used by sailors over the centuries—charts, a compass, a sexton, or in our day, a GPS tracking device. In the same way, you can discover God on your own, apart from any teaching of any church. But you are far more likely to understand what God has revealed himself to be by turning to a teaching that has been accurate and helpful for two thousand years—the Trinity.

Many gods are competing for our attention: wealth, fame, ease, comfort, sex. Only one God deserves our allegiance, God in three persons, blessed Trinity.

## ❁ Fourth Diversion

Transitions are a continuing part of life. Change comes whether we are prepared for it or not, whether we like it or not. Transitions may be positive or negative. They may bring benefits, or they may bring difficulties. They can break us, or they can make us stronger. The way we respond and adapt to life's transitions has much to do with our degree of happiness and our sense of inner contentment. But the transitions will take place, and one way or another, we must adjust to them.

One of life's transitions, which can come at any age, is the death of a parent. Having loving parents is one of life's greatest blessings. The loss of a parent by death or even by abandonment brings pain and a deep sense of loss. Mary Kay and I were extremely blessed to have our parents until well into our adult lives, and they always, always gave us their love and support. My parents died five days apart from one another. Dad became ill with a case of pneumonia, complicated by a previous lung condition. On the eve of the New Year 2002, we managed to have a toast in his hospital room. Dad lifted his glass and said, "To all the good times past; to all the good times still ahead." He died nine days later. Mom was in declining health, both physical and mental, and confined to a nursing facility. She was ready for her earthly life to come to an end. A strong woman of faith, she had no doubt about where she was going. Mary Kay's mother, Gail Hughes Cammack, suffered a debilitating stroke, which left her paralyzed for many years. Her husband, Raymond, became the main caregiver, a job he performed with great patience and personal attention. Always inventive, Ray designed and built a chair-lift device to enable Gail to go up and down stairs in a wheelchair. They were still able to make brief trips in the car and to enjoy the beautiful scenery along the Yellowstone River. Ray outlived Gail, and both are buried near their home, in Carbon County, Montana, in view of the magnificent Rocky Mountains.

Of all life's transitions, becoming a grandparent is surely among the very best. The old wisdom that you can simply enjoy your grandchildren, without the awesome responsibility of raising them, is, in most circumstances, the absolute truth. Mary Kay and I have been blessed beyond any measurement with four grandchildren. Byron and Kristen have two sons, Josiah and Nicholas, and Andrew and Kristen have a son and a daughter, Alexander and Rowan. What a joy to see them grow, go to school, play sports, take music lessons, and to receive the love and joy they have when they greet Grandma and Grandpa. And we consider ourselves especially blessed that they are being raised in homes where faith is a strong part of daily life.

Retirement, too, is one of life's transitions. I have always believed that you should never go from something but always to something. Don't drop out of school unless you have some positive alternative. Don't quit a job unless you have another offer in hand. Don't walk out of a difficult situation or marriage without something better to walk into. So when I retired in June 2010, retirement was short-lived. As we contemplated retirement, Mary Kay said, "Wouldn't it be great to live in Europe for a few years?" She was thinking of a villa in Tuscany, overlooking lush vineyards to the east and the clear blue waters of the Mediterranean on the west. All I heard was Europe. I e-mailed the Methodist Church in Ireland with a simple request: if you have a small church with a manse that needs a pastor, let's talk. They immediately responded: Come on over. I received a two-year appointment to Queen's Parade Methodist Church in Bangor, Northern Ireland, and became their pastor in July 2010.

I had never heard of Bangor, a town fifteen miles east of Belfast. But I quickly learned of its historic significance for the Christian Church. In the mid-500s, a monastery was founded there that became a place of learning and preserving the Scriptures. Saints Columbanus and Gaul went forth from its walls to spread the gospel through large parts of France and Switzerland. Although destroyed by the Vikings, the monastery played a major role in keeping the Christian faith alive in Europe. Within a day's drive of Bangor (driving, of course, on the left side of the road) were sites of Patrick's ministry, megalithic tombs, and spectacular scenery along the Antrim coast. Our manse was just a ten-minute walk from the Irish Sea. We went there daily to walk, pray, see the seabirds, and look across the waters to Scotland, which could be seen in clear weather. And of course, we frequently went to Belfast, where reminders of the Troubles are still very apparent. A large wall still divides Protestant and Catholic neighborhoods, and occasional "petrol bombs" still bring death and devastation. But at no point did we ever feel endangered, and everywhere we went, the Irish people were extremely friendly and gracious.

The experience at Queen's Parade was tremendously enjoyable and enriching. The building had been erected in the early 1800s and had survived two bombs, one in World War II and another during the Troubles. Singing hymns was always a challenge for me, for the small hymnals contained only the words, and the tunes, even to familiar hymns, were often different from what I had known. The congregation welcomed "the wee Americans" with a warm hospitality, and we made close friends there. A special outreach of the church was the weekly seniors' luncheon, when homemade meals were served to senior citizens in the church and community. I peeled countless potatoes at those luncheons, for "champ" (mashed potatoes and scallions) was a frequent staple. Mary Kay shared her considerable cooking skills as well.

We returned to our American home in July 2013, and very quickly, another transition, this one unexpected, took place. I became the interim senior pastor of Trinity United Methodist Church in Prince Frederick, Maryland, for a nine-month period. Once again, we were blessed to be part of a vital congregation, intent on serving the community and offering a meaningful worship experience and a quality program of education. Music at Trinity was quite varied, from classical to blue grass, traditional to praise songs. It seems that the churches I have served have always enriched me far more than I have enriched them, and that was true of Trinity. Though our ministry there was very brief, we left with a deep appreciation for many devoted Christian friends.

Life goes on, and transitions will come. Life is not our own; it is a gift that comes from beyond ourselves. Lord, keep me open to ways to serve you and love you, and, as a wise and loving man once said, to be thankful for all the good times past and for all the good times still ahead.

## Generous to All

How can it be? Some work in the vineyard all day long, sweating, laboring, their muscles aching. Some don't arrive until nine o'clock, several hours after the sun has risen. Some come at noon, some do not show up until midafternoon, and some come strolling in at five o'clock in the evening. And yet at the end of the day, each worker receives an equal amount of pay (Matthew 20:1–16). How unfair! What vineyard owner would be so corrupt and evil? Where is the justice in this parable of Jesus?

What makes Jesus' parable even more shocking is that the vineyard owner is God. The kingdom of heaven is like the vineyard owner (Matthew 20:1). The parable is told in response to Peter's question, "Look, we have left everything and followed you. What then will we have?" (Matthew 19:27). Is Jesus suggesting that God is so blatantly unjust? Will a devoted follower who worships, gives, volunteers, forgives, serves, and sacrifices have the same reward as the dirty, rotten, lowdown scoundrel who may utter a deathbed repentance? The apparent answer is yes! The deathbed convert enters the kingdom of heaven as surely as the exemplary church folks who have been card-carrying believers all their lives.

Where is the justice?

John described his glorious vision of the kingdom of heaven, the New Jerusalem (Revelation 21). He wrote of twelve gates that surround the city: three on the east, three on the north, three on the south, and three on the west (Revelation 21:12–13). The gates are never shut (Revelation

20:25). Could it be that the gates on the east are for those who come early in the morning, at the rising of the sun, in the beginning of their lives? Could it be that the gates in the west are for those who come from the setting sun, at the close of the day, the end of their lives? And the gates will be open! All who come with an open heart, from any direction and at any time, will be welcome.

But again we may ask, where is justice? How can this be fair?

In the parable, each worker is paid one *denarius*. When the parable was told, one *denarius* was the normal daily pay for the average worker. Workers who labored for a day received one *denarius*. Another way of thinking of that is to understand that one *denarius* was the amount of money needed for the average person to put food on the table, buy clothing for the family, and provide a home in which to live. The owner of the vineyard wanted each of his workers to have the daily necessities of life. No one was to go hungry, no one was to be homeless, no one was without adequate provision, and that was to be true no matter how long they may have worked. It is purely a matter of generosity on the part of the vineyard owner. "Am I not allowed to do what I choose with what belongs to me? Or are you envious because I am generous?" (Matthew 20:15).

If you want to know what injustice is, consider the people in today's society who do not have adequate food, housing, medical care, or a retirement plan, even though they work. Injustice is compensation that is inadequate to meet the basic needs of life. The fact that an employee is a kitchen worker, or a trash collector, a mower of lawns, or a cleaner of gutters is no excuse for inadequate pay. Neither is the fact that the employee may be an immigrant from another country. Justice means that all will receive their daily bread.

And then, there is the matter of urgency. The workers in the vineyard are not shuffling papers; they are gathering the harvest. When the crop is ripe in the field or on the tree, it must be harvested. There is a narrow window of time to complete the work. You cannot wait; you must do it now. Near the end of summer, there is a full moon that is called a "harvest moon." I never knew what that meant until my wife, who was raised on a farm, explained it to me. In the old days, a full moon allowed farmers to work late at night, perhaps all night long, to gather the harvest. For the harvest must be gathered, safe and secure. Every hour is precious. Every worker is needed. Even if you come late in the day, there is work for you to do.

It is never too late to render a loving service to God or to another person. It is never too late in the day to show kindness or seek reconciliation. It is never too late in life to love, to forgive, to pray, or to say thank you. Your service is needed and valuable, no matter when it comes.

God wants all his dear children to have adequate provision. God wants all employed in deeds of love and mercy. God wants all to enter into the joy of his eternal kingdom. Never begrudge that kindness, that purpose, that generosity. For it is only by God's grace that anyone is saved.

All are needed. All are wanted. All are important. And God is generous to all.

# ✦ Where is Spain?

"I am longing to see you ..." With a passionate intensity, Paul wrote these words to the Church in Rome (Romans 1:11). Like a child eagerly anticipating the arrival of Christmas, Paul could scarcely wait to arrive in Rome, to give and receive gifts of support and encouragement with cherished friends and fellow Christians (Romans 1:11–12).

But when we read to the end of the letter to the Romans, we discover that Paul had something else in mind. With a telling admission, Paul revealed that he would not stay long in Rome. He would just be passing through. What he really wanted to do was to go to Spain (Romans 15:23–24).

Spain? Why Spain? Did Paul wish to worship in the great cathedrals of Barcelona or Madrid? No. As far as we know, there were no churches in Spain when Paul wrote Romans. There were no Christians there. And that is precisely the point. Paul wanted to go to where there was no church, to a place where people needed to hear the good news of Christ's resurrection. Spain was the last country that Paul knew about. If he had known about North America, he would have written, "I want to go to Spain, and then on to Canada and Mexico and the USA."

Where is Spain today? Where are people who need to hear good news? Where are people, deep in despair and loneliness, who need to know that God has a purpose for each precious individual? Where is the teenager who needs to hear that life is more than the momentary high from popping pills? Where is the divorcee who needs to know that new life is still possible? Where is the cancer patient who needs to understand that love is everlasting and that death cannot shorten the length of eternal life, not even by a moment?

Spain is as far away as the starving child in Sudan, the refugee in a makeshift tent in the Middle East, the political prisoner in a North Korean labor camp, or the family left homeless by a typhoon in Bangladesh. And Spain is as near as the nursing home at the end of the block, the nightly occupied bench in the town park, or the prison cell in the city jail. Spain is a close as your office, your school, your mall, or your home. Spain is wherever the Father's dear children need to hear good news, "the Gospel: it is the power of God for salvation" (Romans 1:16).

We cannot learn of the Easter message of resurrection and sit back in idle disinterest. We cannot hear the summons to love the neighbor and ignore the needs of others. We cannot be summoned to forgive and then remain imprisoned by our bitterness. We cannot witness injustice and pretend that it does not exist. We cannot know of human need and complacently rest in silent isolation. Either we live to ourselves, or we live together in joyful trust and faithfulness. There is no other way, no other choice. We have no power to save, but, like John the Baptist, we can raise our arms and point the way to the Savior: "Here is the Lamb of God, who takes away the sins of the world!" (John 1:29).

Don't take time to call your travel agent.

Just go to Spain.

# ◈ Confidence

I am not an alumnus of the University of Maryland, but I am a fan of Maryland basketball. I am a nervous, nail-biting, edge-of-my-seat fan, especially when the games are close and are not decided until the last few seconds.

One day, I watched a game on television that was tension-filled from beginning to end. The lead kept changing back and forth, and with less than a minute to play, Maryland lost the lead. The television cameras panned the arena, and you could see the worry on the faces of the fans. On the Maryland bench, some players sat with towels over their heads; they could not bear to watch the closing seconds. Normally, that is the way that I am but not this game. I sat relaxed in my chair, perfectly at peace. I knew that my team was going to win. I just knew it! I had complete confidence that Maryland would win the game. And they won!

How could I be so confident in such a tension-filled time? It was a delayed telecast. The game had been played earlier that day, and I already knew the final score.

The promise of resurrection is like that. The hope of eternal life is not a vague wish or a passing dream. It is a certainty. The contest between life and death has already been won.

One day, a synagogue leader came to Jesus with a desperate plea: his daughter was dying (Mark 5:21–43). Jesus accompanied the man to his home, but before they arrived, the girl died. The wailing and weeping of extreme grief had already begun. Jesus entered the room of death and took the girl by the hand. With a voice of absolute command he spoke, *"Tabitha, cum"* (Mark 5:41). Now, *"tabitha cum"* is Aramaic, a surprising and notable phrase in the Greek text of the Gospel of Mark. Why the Aramaic in a Greek text? It is a sign of authenticity; it is what Jesus actually said. Mark explains to his Greek readers that *"tabitha cum"* means "Little girl, arise." And the little girl got up and walked about.

That same voice of command will one day speak again, and death and Hades will give up their dead (Revelation 20:13), and death will be no more (Revelation 21:4). One day we shall hear that voice: Little girl, arise. Little boy, arise. And we shall be raised up.

Count on it! The Lord of life will do it!

# ❁ I Want You to Know

Some things take time. It takes time to become fluent in a foreign language. It takes time to acquire proficiency in a sport. It takes time to excel in playing a musical instrument. It takes time to develop a good wine. And it takes time to move through grief.

Grief is a common and normal experience. Everyone reading these words has known grief, or is now grieving some loss, or will one day do so. When we have much to grieve, we have much pain to bear. Sorrow and an overwhelming sense of loss, confusion and the inability to function normally, anger and guilt—all are part of the suffering that accompanies grief. And it all takes time. Each person must go through grief in his or her own time and in his or her own way. If you have friends in grief, be very sensitive to them. Do not rush them, and do not send them on a guilt trip because they are not progressing according to your expectations. And when you are in grief, be patient. Moving through grief is not a steady, linear improvement; it is a series of ups and downs, of experiencing a day of normal activities and suddenly being crushed in despair, of laughter intermingled with tears. It is not easy. You cannot lose someone dear without experiencing suffering and pain.

For everyone who has suffered, or now suffers, or ever will suffer in grief, Paul has an important message: "But we do not want you to be uninformed, brothers and sisters, about those who have died, so that you may not grieve as others do who have no hope. For since we believe that Jesus died and rose again, even so, through Jesus, God will bring with him those who have died" (1 Thessalonians 4:13–14).

We all grieve. We must all say good-bye to loved ones, and saying good-bye is not easy. We lose too much not to grieve. But I want you to know something, Paul writes. I want you to know so you will not grieve as those who have no hope. I want you to know the truth about those who have died. And what is that truth? The truth is that Jesus Christ died but rose again, and that through Jesus, God will give new life to all who belong to him. "And so we will be with the Lord forever" (1 Thessalonians 4:17b).

Christian hope is not just wishful thinking. It is not some scatterbrained idea based upon a sentimental notion that somehow, somewhere there may be a life after death. It is grounded in Jesus Christ and in his resurrection. It is based on the mighty act of God in raising Jesus from the dead and in the certainty that Christ will keep his promise: "because I live, you also will live" (John 14:19b).

The bottom line is that Jesus Christ is Lord. He is Lord over all nations and governments and political systems. He is Lord over all powers and forces. He is Lord over all sickness and suffering and pain. He is Lord over the power of sin. And he is Lord over death.

God is on his throne. He is God when we are alive, and he is God when we have gone from this earth. Our future is secure in him, the very One who gave us life to begin with, who brought us forth from the dust of the earth and breathed into us the breath of life (Genesis 2:7). We need not be afraid.

We have much to grieve, but we do not grieve as those who have no hope. We have much to be thankful for.

I just wanted you to know.

# Out of a Tomb

Jesus was crucified, dead, and buried. He was sealed in a cold, dark tomb. A big, big stone was placed in front of the entry. Early in the morning of the third day, grieving women came to anoint his body with oils and spices. They asked themselves, "Who will roll away the stone for us from the entrance of the tomb?" (Mark 16:3). They had come to pay their last respects to poor old dead Jesus, sealed in a tomb.

Actually, it is pretty comfortable that way, with Jesus dead and sealed in a tomb. If Jesus is sealed in a tomb, we don't have to deal with him. He makes no claim upon our lives, no demands upon our time and talents and energies. If Jesus stays dead, we don't have to deal with all that stuff about loving your enemy, forgiving others, feeding the hungry, or caring for the needy. If Jesus is in the grave, we can ignore that talk about turning the other cheek, entering by the narrow gate, being the salt of the earth and the light of the world, and seeking first the kingdom of God and his righteousness. If Jesus were contained behind a big stone, we could visit the site, lay some flowers, place a wreath, and get on with our lives.

But we can't. When the women arrived at the tomb, it was empty. By the mighty act of God, Jesus was made alive. It was not Jesus who is dead; it was death that is dead. The good news of resurrection does not mean that the spirit of Jesus lives on, like the spirit of Abraham Lincoln or Martin Luther King Jr. lives on in the continuing effort for racial equality. It is not a metaphor that somehow hope lives on or that spring will return. The resurrection of Jesus is real and true, the mighty power of God breaking into this world to vindicate his righteousness and to defeat the dominion of sin and death for evermore.

The resurrection does not mean that someone was raised from the dead. Jesus was raised from the dead. He who was born in a stable amid animals and straw, he who came teaching love and goodness, he who stood for justice and righteousness, he who ate and drank with tax collectors and sinners, he who struggled up a hill with a cross on his back, *he* was raised by the mighty act of God. And in his resurrection, a new creation has begun.

The tomb could not hold him in. He broke out of the tomb. And because he broke out of the tomb, we can break out of ours.

Is it not the case that we need to break out of our tombs? Are we not enclosed in our own self-made tombs? The tomb is not a very pleasant place to be. It is cold and dark and lonely in our tombs, our deep, deep tombs behind big, big stones, where we are isolated and rejected. What tomb do you need to break out of?

Perhaps we need to break out of the tomb of doubt. We think it must be too good to be true. Like Thomas, we insist on empirical proof. "Unless I see the mark of the nails in his hands, and put my finger in the mark of the nails and my hand in his side, I will not believe" (John 20:25). But is that doubt? Or does that not sound more like pride—a defiant, arrogant, and self-righteous pride? If we could lay aside our pride, our doubt would disappear as well. Let go of the pride, trust in the good news, and break out of your tomb.

Perhaps you are in the tomb of worry. There is so much in this world to be anxious about, so many fears to contend with. Can you not see that all the worry in the world does you no good whatsoever and may even be the cause of harm? Can you not understand that worry is a subtle but insidious form of atheism, for it calls into doubt the ultimate sovereignty and grace of the Father? Trust that God's ultimate purpose for your life will be fulfilled, regardless of what may happen in this passing world. Don't be afraid to offer your worry to the One who reveals himself as love. Open your heart to a presence that is with us always, even to the close of the age (Matthew 28:20). And break out of your tomb.

Perhaps, like most of us, it is not just one tomb that holds you in but many tombs. Despair, bitterness, the failure to forgive, the unwillingness to accept forgiveness, the self-imposed need to seek revenge, the addiction to drink, drugs, or gambling—all are deep and isolating tombs, and all are a form of dying before our natural death. Perhaps it is tomb of mediocrity, settling for a life that is unfocused, uncommitted, and unfulfilled. Or perhaps we are in the tomb of religion itself, if religion represents legalisms and bigotry and arguments over philosophical doctrines. We go from one tomb to another. From tomb to tomb we seem to go.

But we can break out of our tombs. For faith is more than a mental belief in certain theological dogmas; it is a sure and certain reliance on the grace of God. It brings inner peace and calls for a response of grateful and joyful obedience.

Christ is alive! He has broken out of the tomb! And because he lives, we shall live also (John 14:19). Believe me when I say, there is no tomb. There is no tomb, not the self-imposed tombs that we create and not the tomb that will contain our remains when this earthly life ends. There is no tomb that can hold us in.

## ❁ Becoming

What is it? My son and I were completely mystified as we looked upon it, a small piece of clear plastic containing a slot with a hole in it, and two prongs that protruded out from one of its several flat sides. We had no idea what it was, this strange little whatchamacallit in the Hallmark Visitors Center in downtown Kansas City, Missouri. We had taken my grandchildren to Kaleidoscope, a marvelous facility that contains bins filled with crayons, magic markers, paper of every size and shape, ribbons, and little craft items—everything a child could possibly want to create a work of art. Finally, our curiosity could not be contained. We took the small plastic piece to one of the staff members, held it forth, and asked, "What is it?" The answer we received was memorable. "Here at Kaleidoscope, we don't ask what it is. We only ask what it might become."

Is that not precisely the way that God looks upon us?

When God looked down upon the Hebrew people enslaved in Egypt, God did not ask, "What are they?" The answer to that question was obvious: they are slaves. They have no wealth, no assets, no property, no education, no training, no technology, no army, no power. They are nobodies. But God did not ask what they were. God asked what they might become. They might become a holy nation (Exodus 19:6). They might become the bearers of moral law (Exodus 20:1–17). They might become a light for the Gentiles (Isaiah 49:6). And from their kings there might descend a Messiah, the Savior of the world (Matthew 1:1).

Gideon was threshing grain in a cellar. It was hard enough to thresh grain outside, with dirt and dust in your lungs and in your eyes. And

Gideon was threshing in a cellar, because Midianites were in the land, oppressing the Hebrew people and stealing their grain. When God looked down upon this pathetic scene, God did not ask what Gideon was. The answer to that question was obvious: Gideon was a scared and yellow-bellied coward, the least of his clan. God asked what Gideon might become—a man with so much faith that he would he would go into battle against the Midianite army, with a band of three hundred men whose weapons were torches and earthenware jars (Judges 6:11–16; 7:1–23).

When God looked down upon Jeremiah, God did not ask, "Who is he?" The answer to that question was obvious: he was a teenager. He had not graduated from high school. He had no degree, no experience, nothing to commend him. Instead, God asked what Jeremiah might become: a great prophet, a revealer of hope and truth, a man who would proclaim that the day is coming when there would be a new covenant, not written on stone but written on the heart (Jeremiah 1:4–8; 31:31–34).

A young man, living in a pigpen, wasted and destitute, realized that he would be better off as a servant in his father's house and decided to go home. His father saw him coming from a distance. The father did not ask, "Who is it?" The answer to that question was obvious: he was a worthless and miserable wretch who had squandered the father's estate. The father asked what the boy might become: a restored son, sitting at the father's table. So the father put a ring on his finger and shoes on his feet and hosted the biggest party the lad had ever seen (Luke 15:11–32).

I might look into my life and see that I have made a mess of things. I might think, "I am a loser. I have failed. I have fallen short. I have made mistakes. I have sinned greatly." And I might be absolutely correct. I might really be a loser. Like the man who went to the psychiatrist and said, "Doctor, I have an inferiority complex." And the doctor replied, "It is not a complex. You really are inferior." But what I might be is not the issue. The issue is what I might become.

I might look around at others. I might see neighbors, colleagues, kids in my school, even my own family members who have ruined their lives. I might see alcoholics, drug abusers, those who are addicted to pornography or who have wasted their resources in casinos. I might see cheaters, liars, slanderers, or people driven by greed, lust, or envy, filled with arrogance or contempt. They are losers, through and through. I need not ask what they are; the answer is obvious. I need to ask what they might become.

Never, never, never, never, never give up on someone else. And never, never, never, never, never give up on yourself.

For in Christ there is the power to become a new creation (2 Corinthians 5:17). The old has passed away; the new has come.

Do not ask, "What is it?"

Only ask what it might become.

#  The Invitation

Even seasoned fishermen can be frightened by a storm at sea. When the winds are pushing you farther and farther off course, when swelling waves come crashing down on your little boat, and when you must grasp at a rope to keep from being swept into the deep, it is a terrifying moment.

So it was for the disciples of Jesus, late one night, struggling in the stormy darkness to keep their small craft afloat. Fear turned to panic as one of them, peering out across the turbulent waters, thought he saw a figure moving straight toward them. One of them thought it might be Jesus, but that, of course, would have been impossible. Surely it must be a ghost! Peter cried out to see if was really the Lord. Jesus answered, "It is I," or at least that is what the English translations say. In the Greek text, Jesus answers *ego eimi*—"I am." I AM, the name of God in the Hebrew Scripture. Is it you, Lord? I AM, Peter. I AM. Come to me.

Let no one think this is only a story of two thousand years ago. We are the fisherman in that little boat. We are separated from Jesus by twenty centuries of time, separated by the darkness of doubts and skepticism and separated by the fears and worries of the storms that can so quickly arise and trouble the waters of our lives. Is Jesus really there? Has he really risen from the dead? Can he help me? Can he save me? Can he deliver me from sin and from death? Or is he just an apparition, a wish projection of insecure and fearful people who must live in a stormy world, knowing they are going to die? Is he real? Or is he but a ghost?

Could it be that Jesus' answer to Peter is the answer he gives to us? Come to me. Come now; come this very minute. Do not delay another moment. Let not your little boat be lost in the abyss of sin and death, but come to me. Experience me, live in me, trust in me, and give yourself over to me. Love as I love, live as I live, and follow in my way, and then you will know that I AM. Not I *was*, but I AM. I am real. I am alive. I shall live forevermore, and my love will never end.

Only you can answer the invitation of Jesus, Come to me. Your mother or father cannot answer for you. Your neighbor on the left or the right cannot answer for you. Do not look to others to make the decision on your behalf. Across the reluctant fears, across the nagging doubts, and across the stormy waters, the invitation comes. Only you can answer.

Let no one think that Jesus is speaking to someone else.

# From Above

He was a good man, a very good man. He studied Holy Scripture at great length and honestly tried to put its teachings into daily practice. Carefully, he carried out even the most minute of the religious customs and rituals of his day. He was there when the synagogue services took place—praying, learning, and teaching. He was part of a group that tithed with great precision, meticulously giving a tenth not only of his money but even of the mint, dill, and cumin that he grew in his small garden (Matthew 23:23). And he was educated, sophisticated, and able to converse intelligently about the events of the day (John 3:2). Though a leader of his Jewish people, he bore a Greek name, Nicodemus, suggesting he was raised in a family that could easily relate to people of another culture and belief (John 3:1).

He came to Jesus by night (John 3:2). He came by stealth in the cover of darkness, perhaps because he did not want to risk the disapproval and ridicule of his colleagues. It was easier not to be seen coming to Jesus, as indeed, many in the modern world may wish to keep their faith a secret. It is easier to keep it to oneself and not to talk about it in the workplace or at a cocktail party. Or perhaps he came to Jesus in the darkness of the soul, with fears, uncertainties, inner conflicts, and doubts. Perhaps he came, realizing he had a deep need but without understanding what the need was or how to find fulfillment. Perhaps he was simply "in the dark." In any event, he is not merely a figure from the ancient world; he lives in our time and in our world. He may be found by simply looking around. And he may be found by looking down inside, into our own inner lives.

Even in the darkness, Jesus was there and will be there, ready to receive, to talk, to relate, and to welcome. Nicodemus, he said, what is needed is not more knowledge, not more information, not more piety, not more of religion, and not more churchliness—not more anything. What is needed is an transformation of life that is so complete and so absolute that it can only be described as being born anew (John 3:3). It is not your being religious that makes you worthy in God's sight. It is not your being good, not your being pious, not your being obedient to every letter of the law, not your mastery of all the proper doctrines and rituals, and most certainly not your ability to give a cogent explanation as to why people of every other religion are wrong. What matters is being born from above.

What Jesus said to Nicodemus he says to us and to all who walk in darkness. Grace is offered to you; receive it. Forgiveness is being given; accept it. New life is open to you; grab hold of it. I welcome you to a realm of love; indeed, to a kingdom of infinite glory. Believe it, rely upon it, and claim it as your own.

Do we not hear the renewing power of Jesus' message? Come to me, Nicodemus. Come to me, men, women, and children of every place and time. Come to me. Forget about your good works. Forget about your ceremonies, your interpretations, and your dogmas. Forget about the distinctions that set you apart and make you different. Come to me. Let your spirit be open to my spirit. Let your life be changed by the power of everlasting life. Let my love be the center of your being and of all that you do and work for.

And to all who come, it will be as if they were born anew. They will be "born, not of blood of the will of the flesh or of the will of man, but of God" (John 1:13). They will be born from above.

# ✺ A Day in Early March

Early March is a dreary time of year, with a drab shabbiness to the wintry landscape. Winter in March is not a scene of evergreens blanketed in the beauteous whiteness of a fresh and newly fallen snow. Winter in March is lifeless trees and barren fields. Here and there in the secluded shadows, piles of snow may yet remain, no longer pure and lovely but dirty and encrusted with soot. The air is still cold. The rays of the sun are distant and oblique to the surface of the earth. A bitter northern wind pierces the coat and chills to the very bone. Mostly, there is mud—mud everywhere—clinging to the shoes and tracking in upon the carpet.

Our little day in time can be like that. The personal pains and sufferings, the evils and injustices of the world around us, the anxieties and the fears, the constant reality of insecurity, and the sharp grief of a recent loss all may seem so intense and so persistent that we may wonder if anything could ever check their power. Death and decay pervade our thoughts. All of life may appear to be ugly and bleak, like the steel-gray skies of a day in early March.

And what becomes of faith and hope in such an environment? The nonbelieving mockers may pierce through our thin lines of defense. God is a delusion, they tell us, and religious people are but ignorant and unscientific morons. With contempt and scorn, they attack religious institutions as endangered species from a bygone age that soon will be no more. And when faith, with all its evils and superstitions, becomes extinct, it will be good riddance to a way of thinking that both limits human progress and is dangerous to the very core.

Such is our despair when all of life is like a day in early March.

But if we take a closer look at the early March landscape, we receive a very different impression. If we push away the layers of rotten leaves, we notice little shoots of green springing up out of the earth. In protected corners, crocuses and daffodils are bursting forth in blooms of gold and purple. From the tips of branches, germinal buds prepare to erupt in foliage. Suddenly, the lawn is brightened by the flash of a robin's breast. High overhead, we may hear the honks of geese, returning to their summer homes. Even the brown grass is changing to a light and verdant green. And suddenly, we realize that we are standing on the brink of an incredible transformation: winter is passing away, and spring is breaking forth upon the hemisphere. A miracle is unfolding before our eyes. Yes, a miracle. For a miracle is not a trick of magic and not merely a supernatural oddity. Miracles are signs of mighty acts of God, bringing grace to a fallen world.

"Your kingdom come, Your will be done," we pray, and surely it is coming (Matthew 6:10). Even now, it has dawned upon us, and its fulfillment will not be delayed. Not by our feeble witness, our weak faith, our faltering obedience, or our casual indifference will it come, but by the mighty act of a Sovereign God. That kingdom will come as surely as the spring will replace the winter, and the rising sun will dispel the nighttime darkness.

Our little place in space and time may resemble the desolate landscape of early March, but it will not always be so. One day, flowers will bloom upon the earth. One day, the great flights of the wild geese will lift up from their watery bed and head majestically home. One day, the warming sun will bathe this world in newness of life. We know not when, but one day it will happen. Who cannot discern its dawning? "The time is fulfilled; the Kingdom of God is near; turn away from your sin and believe the good news" (Mark 1:15).

We are passing out of death and into life (John 5:24). We are living in a day in early March.

# ✸ Like Christ

Economists speak of the law of insatiable demands. We want more and more. We never have enough. If we have a mansion, we want a bigger mansion—or at least the addition of a new sunroom. If we have a car, no matter how costly, we want two cars, the second as luxurious as the first. No matter how large our inventory of assets, we want more stocks to add to the portfolio. It is our human condition to constantly want more than what we have.

Our problem is not that we want too much. Our problem is that we want too little.

We are satisfied with material possessions when we could have riches that this world cannot take away. We are content with mediocrity, when greatness can be ours. We cheat ourselves when we do not strive to become the very noblest and highest that we can be. We settle for acting like everyone else, when we have the potential to be like Christ.

The purpose of the Christian Church is to make people like Christ. All the sermons and all the liturgies and all the trappings will mean nothing if the church does not make people to be like Christ. To make me like Christ. To make you like Christ.

To be like Christ is not simply to avoid the obnoxious sins and scandalous behaviors. It is more than being a nice guy or a decent woman, a good little boy or a sweet little girl. To be like Christ is to allow Christ to come into our lives and take control. It is to let Christ work through these human instruments we call our lives, so that our words are what Christ would say, and our deeds are what Christ would do.

To be like Christ is to be set free from the worry of how we will survive from day to day, set free from the bondage of death, and know the glorious freedom of the children of God (Romans 8:21). To be like Christ is to be healed from the poison of vengeful bitterness and to live in peace and harmony with others (Romans 12:18–19). To be like Christ is to love the Lord your God with all your heart, with all your soul, and with all your mind and to love your neighbor as yourself (Matthew 22:37–39).

It does not matter what you have been in the past. It does not matter what sin you have committed, what broken relationships you have suffered, what disappointment you have known, or what failures you have experienced. It does not matter what abundant affluence you have known or what poverty you have endured. Even at this very moment, you can choose to become like Christ, to accept his grace, and to begin to walk in the new life he freely offers.

Why would you settle for anything less?

## Keep the Faith

It was a day of play for me, a day of work for my grandfather. I was just a little guy. We had gone to the home of my great-grandmother, now quite aged. Grandpa worked, doing the countless odd jobs that are needed to maintain a house and lawn, while I played. At the end of the day, he took me by the hand and led me past the old barn, now used only as a storage place for old garden tools. An owl had made her home near the peak of the old wooden rafters. We kept walking, along a path where wild blackberries grew, to the crest of a small hill. There, we sat and watched the sun go down. As it slowly sank beneath the horizon, my grandfather told stories from the past, remembrances that were precious to him. And the sun went down on another day.

Generations come and generations go—great-grandparents, grandparents, moms and dads, children, grandchildren, great-grandchildren. Each generation must pass on to the next the values, beliefs, and traditions that it holds dear. Each generation must pass on the things that matter most. It may be a wedding ring worn by a grandparent, a pocket watch long since made obsolete, a piece of furniture worn through years of use, items of little value in an auction but rich in memories. And along with its possessions, each generation must pass on the things of greater worth—its stories, its remembrances, and its faith.

Near the end of his life, Paul made a personal plea to a younger follower of the Christ: "Timothy, guard what has been entrusted to you" (1 Timothy 6:20). Keep the faith, Timothy. Whatever else you do, keep the faith. Hold it fast. Preserve it. Protect it. Share it. Pass it on. Keep alive the pre-eminence of love, the demand for justice, and the hope of eternal life.

It is our privilege and challenge to be keepers of the faith. Do not take that mission lightly. We must tell the story. We must live the gospel. We must let others see the presence of Christ in our lives.

There are many ways to pass on a precious treasure. Perhaps it can be done in so simple a way as this: take your grandchild by the hand, walk to the top of a little rise, and sit and talk together.

And watch the sun go down on another day.

## ❂ Daffodils

From the thawing ground they emerge, prophets of a coming spring, pioneers of others that are yet to come—dogwood, azalea, wisteria, and myrtle. How bold they are, these golden bursts that stand defiant against a flurried snow and bone-chilled wind. And yet how infinitely complex they are, their delicate curled blossoms surrounding microscopic grains of pollen on a heaven-pointed shaft. Not limited to the cultivated gardens of human habitation, they break forth in a thousand places at woodland's edge and in the meadows fair. They have caused a despairing poet, wandering lonely as a cloud, to join their fluttering dance. And they can bring a joy unknown to minds of winter darkness.

In all my life, in all the sermons I have ever preached, and in all the classes I have ever taught, if I even once glorified the Creator as fully and as profoundly as a single daffodil, my life would be fulfilled. More than fulfilled, it would be an offering.

CPSIA information can be obtained at www.ICGtesting.com
Printed in the USA
LVOW06s1415010614

388104LV00002B/523/P